Warrior • 73

Osprey

C000173101

Tito's Partisans 1941–45

Velimir Vuksic

First published in Great Britain in 2003 by Osprey Publishing, Elms Court, Chapel Way, Botley, Oxford OX2 9LP, United Kingdom.
Email: info@ospreypublishing.com

A CIP catalogue record for this book is available from the British Library.

ISBN 1 84176 675 5

Editor: Tom Lowres
Design: Ken Vail Graphic Design, Cambridge, UK
Index by Alan Thatcher
Originated by The Electronic Page Company, Cwmbran, UK
Printed in China through World Print Ltd.

03 04 05 06 07 10 9 8 7 6 5 4 3 2 1

FOR A CATALOGUE OF ALL BOOKS PUBLISHED BY OSPREY MILITARY AND AVIATION PLEASE CONTACT:

Osprey Direct UK, P.O. Box 140, Wellingborough, Northants, NN8 2FA, UK
E-mail: info@ospreydirect.co.uk

Osprey Direct USA, c/o MBI Publishing, P.O. Box 1, 729 Prospect Ave, Osceola, WI 54020, USA
E-mail: info@ospreydirectusa.com

www.ospreypublishing.com

Artist's note

Readers may care to note that the original paintings from which the colour plates in this book were prepared are available for private sale. All reproduction copyright whatsoever is retained by the Publishers. All enquiries should be addressed to:

Velimir Vuksic,
Ilica 54,
Zagreb,
10,000,
Croatia

The Publishers regret that they can enter into no correspondence upon this matter.

Author's note

All photographs appear with kind permission from:

Croatian Historical Museum,
Hrvatski Povijesni Muzej,
Matoseva 9,
10,000 Zagreb,
Croatia

FRONT COVER A Partisan poses with an Italian Breda Modello 65mm light machine gun.
(Croatian Historical Museum)

CONTENTS

TITO'S PARTISANS 1941–45

INTRODUCTION

In 1941, prior to the outbreak of World War II, the Kingdom of Yugoslavia had a little over 16 million inhabitants and covered an area about twice the size of Austria. The largest ethnic group was the Serbs, about six and a half million strong, living in the area of the former Kingdom of Serbia, Kingdom of Montenegro and the newly created States of Croatia, Bosnia and Hercegovina and Macedonia. The Serbs were Orthodox Christians: they used the Cyrillic script and culturally looked to the east of Europe. Serbia was historically close to Tsarist Russia, and Russia helped the Kingdom of Serbia in its 19th-century struggle to create a national state. During World War I the Kingdom of Serbia was Allied to the Western powers, which later assured it good political, economic and military relations with France and Great Britain. The Yugoslav government, state administration and state bank were located in Belgrade, the present Serbian capital, which led the minorities to consider that Serbs dominated the country.

The first official photo of Tito, taken in 1942, and disseminated to all Partisans. Josip Broz Tito (1892–1980) was Supreme Commander of the Partisans and later president for life of Yugoslavia. From 1910 he undertook an apprenticeship as a locksmith and sometime later became a member of the Croatian Social-Democratic Party, the beginning of his political career. During World War I he fought in the Austro-Hungarian Army. He was seriously wounded and became a Russian prisoner of war. He took part in the October Revolution and joined Yugoslav communists in Russia. He returned to Yugoslavia and from 1920 was active as a party and trade union leader and rose up the political hierarchy of the KPJ. In 1928 he was given a five-year prison sentence because of his political activities. After serving this he adopted the name of Tito and began underground political work that drew him ever closer to the Soviet Union: backed by Moscow, in 1940 he became General Secretary of the KPJ. Immediately following the German attack on the USSR in June 1941, the KPJ central committee formed the High Command of the National Liberation Army of Yugoslavia of which Tito was nominated Supreme Commander. In a covert meeting in Belgrade on 4 July Tito and the KPJ called on the constituent nations and people of Yugoslavia to begin an armed uprising. The first battles began soon afterwards. Recent research in Russian historical archives has shown that Stalin sent a directive to Tito to call for an armed uprising. During the war Tito showed himself to be a successful and capable leader: he later became head of the Yugoslav Army which was based on the Soviet model. Historically he is also remembered as a leader who dared to oppose Stalin in the years following the war, as Yugoslavia developed its independent brand of communism.

Map legend:

- - - - - Italian-German demarcation line

INDEPENDENT STATE OF CROATIA (NDH)

Slovenia and Dalmatia annexed by Italy
Montenegro under Italain governor
Kosovo annexed by Italian "Great Albania"

Serbia occupied by Germany

The second largest group was the Croats, numbering a little less than three million people and living in the north-western part of Yugoslavia and within a wide area of current-day Hercegovina. Politically and territorially they were part of Austro-Hungary until the end of World War I. Culturally and historically the Croats looked to Western Europe and the Mediterranean: they were Catholic and used the Latin script. Croatia traditionally had good relationships with Germany and Italy and was under their political influence for many years before World War II.

The third largest group comprised the one and a half million Slovenes, whose historical capital city was Ljubljana. They occupied northern Yugoslavia and had borders with Italy and Austria. Like the Croats, they had been part of the Austro-Hungarian empire and aligned themselves with Western culture: they were Catholic and used the Latin script. They too were under the strong political influence of Italy and Germany. Montenegro had some 400,000 inhabitants, who in terms of culture and religion were very similar to the Serbs. All four of these ethnic groups spoke a common language, although there were regional variations.

Situated on the territory of today's Bosnia and Hercegovina was the Kingdom of Bosnia, a medieval power that had been conquered by the

A German military police unit on a dangerous mountain path. In the high mountains such paths were usually the only way of getting from one village to another.

Ottoman Turks in the mid-15th century. Most of the Croats and Serbs living there converted to Islam while others fled further west to Croatia and Slovenia. Ottoman rule continued in Bosnia until the end of the 19th century when the area was annexed by Austro-Hungary. In the years following World War I the Yugoslav government never acknowledged the muslims in Bosnia as a separate ethnic group and demanded they declare themselves Serbs or Croats. A similar situation arose with the Macedonians, who were Orthodox Christians like the Serbs, and who could not declare themselves as a separate cultural group until after World War II.

Other ethnic minorities included (in order of size): Germans, Austrians, Albanians, Italians, Hungarians and Romanians. There were about half a million Germans and Austrians and the majority of them were expelled to Germany or Austria after World War II.

Two-thirds of the population of Yugoslavia were farmers, making agriculture the cornerstone of the national economy. Control of the national economy was largely in the hands of foreigners, especially French investors.

It is of significance that the most important physical feature of the Balkans, as a scene of military operations, was its rugged terrain. Mountainous and forested areas offered troops numerous places to hide, opportunities to shift forces unseen and locations for ambush.

The national question

After World War I new nation states were created in the territory of the shattered Austro-Hungarian empire. The idea to unite the Slavs in one state, and the fear that Italy, Austria and Hungary might seize part of their national territory, led the Slovenes and Croats in 1918 to unite with the victorious powers from World War I, the kingdoms of Serbia and Montenegro, and create a new country called the Kingdom of Serbs, Croats and Slovenes. The new state was ruled by a parliament and the Serbian king.

The most sensitive region of the new country was Croatia, with a powerful parliamentary battle fought by the Croatian nationalist parties against the hegemony of the Serbian bourgeois. This political battle, called the 'Croatian Question' reached its climax when a member of the Serbian radical party killed Stjepan Radic, president of the largest Croatian party HSS (*Hrvatska Seljacka Stranka*), and injured another man in the Parliament on 8 August 1928. Following this assassination, all political relations between the Croatian and Serbian parties were broken off. Seeing no other way to preserve the position of the court and the Serbian bourgeois, the King decreed on 6 January 1929 that a dictatorship should be instituted. The King also decreed a series of new laws officially renaming the Kingdom of Serbs, Croats and Slovenes the Kingdom of Yugoslavia.

The state was divided into eight new administrative districts. This was aimed at breaking the administration at the national levels in order to strengthen the central government in Belgrade. According to the new divisions, the integral territory of Croatia was administratively split among four territorial divisions. The use of any national flags was strictly prohibited, and with the name change, the state wanted to prove that only one nation lived in the country – the Yugoslavs. The dictatorship and violence assisted the strengthening of various separatist, terrorist and fascist organisations. These organisations worked towards destroying the state, and received assistance from neighbouring countries.

The State Administration, Army and Police were all in Serbian hands thus deepening the antagonism of the non-Serbian peoples towards the state. The Croatian emigrant movement in Italy grew stronger and its political programme was to divide Croatia from Yugoslavia. In 1934, it assassinated the Serbian king in France. However, when Hitler took power, the German influence in the Balkans increased and national tensions declined somewhat.

Due to the events in Europe and the foreign dangers threatening Yugoslavia, the ruling structures sought ways to resolve the situation in the country. In August 1939, an agreement was reached with the HSS, whose members joined the parliament, and according to the new territorial divisions, Croatia received some small autonomous rights. In fact, this was a political agreement between the Croatian and Serbian bourgeois, which failed to resolve the national and other pressing social issues. This situation suited the emigrants, whose programmes of an independent state and national loathing for the Serbs continued to attract new sympathisers.

Ustasha wearing the black uniforms that earned them the name the 'Black Legion'. There was very fierce fighting between the Partisans and the Ustasha. It was waged mercilessly and usually without prisoners being taken. Both sides fought to the last man rather than surrender.

The rise of the Communist Party of Yugoslavia

In the chaos following the demise of the Austro-Hungarian empire, a large number of companies in Slovenia and Croatia collapsed, creating mass unemployment and an economic crisis which developed into one of the greatest problems facing the new state. Peasants began a struggle to acquire land, attacking and plundering the estates and properties of large landowners. Dissatisfaction spread to the streets with a movement that demanded an independent republic. With the arrival of Serbian troops in Croatia and Slovenia tension was defused. In 1919 the social-democratic parties of Serbia, Croatia, Slovenia, Bosnia and Hercegovina, Montenegro and Macedonia united around a programme to reject capitalism and introduce socialist government. In local and state elections held on 28 September 1920 the new Communist Party of Yugoslavia (KPJ) won a significant number of parliamentary seats. In fear of the rise of communism, the government prohibited strikes and suspended the local communist administration that had won the elections. As of 1 August 1921 the functioning of the KPJ was prohibited by law. It is of some interest to note that in 1926 the KPJ's political manifesto was national equality and religious tolerance, and the creation of five federal republics – Serbia, Croatia, Slovenia, Macedonia and Montenegro – with each having the right to become independent. However, after Hitler came to power in 1933, anti-fascism became the KPJ's chief concern. The king and the government banned the KPJ, and party members were imprisoned and given long-term sentences.

The outbreak of war, April 1941

When Hitler attacked Poland in 1939 the Yugoslav government declared its neutrality: following the sudden collapse of France in 1940 it sought to strengthen its ties with Germany. German troops invaded Romania and Hitler gave Yugoslavia an ultimatum of entering the anti-British 'Tripartite Pact' with Romania and Bulgaria or facing the consequences. The massing of German troops on the Bulgarian border accelerated the accession of Bulgaria and Yugoslavia to the pact, which was signed in March 1941. When this became public, demonstrations took place in Belgrade led by the KPJ. The government was toppled and replaced by a new one which rejected the agreement with Germany, thus provoking Hitler's wrath and the outbreak of war. On 6 April 1941 the German Army attacked the Kingdom of Yugoslavia, starting with a heavy air bombardment of Belgrade. The obsolete Yugoslav Army could do little to oppose the German armoured attack especially since many Croats and Slovenes had avoided being drafted or simply refused to fight. Within two weeks Yugoslavia had been overrun and the army laid down its arms. The king and key members of the government fled the country and formed the Yugoslav government in exile, based in London. It is interesting that the German reports on taking over Sarajevo mention the first fighting between Serbs and Croats. When the lightning war ended, Croatian prisoners among the Yugoslav soldiers were allowed to return home while some of them, mostly Serbs, ended up in captivity in Germany. The Balkan fighting postponed the German attack on the Soviet Union for six weeks, which may perhaps have been a decisive factor in the war on the Eastern Front.

The occupation of Yugoslavia

Soon after the invasion, German troops hurriedly left Yugoslavia to prepare for the attack on the Soviet Union. In line with an earlier agreement between Germany and Italy, Yugoslavia was divided into two occupational zones, the German part being twice the size of the Italian part. The Germans handed control of their part of the occupied territory along the Hungarian border to Hungary, and the part in

Macedonia down to the Vardar river valley to Bulgaria. Four weak infantry divisions, the military police and several reserve battalions were responsible for the occupation of the German zone. Almost half of the territory of Yugoslavia was occupied by the Italians, who annexed the best part of the coast and the islands of Dalmatia. The Italian occupation area extended from the coast in the south bordering Albania to a line between the Alps in the north and Lake Prespan on the Greek border. The Italians installed military police and eight divisions to occupy this zone. The Germans retained control of bauxite mining in the Italian zone. In December 1941, foreign occupation forces consisted of 280,000 Italians, 120,000 Germans, 70,000 Bulgarians, and 40,000 Hungarians.

Once the German Army had entered the Croatian capital Zagreb, a puppet regime was installed in the newly defined Independent State of Croatia (NDH), headed by Ante Pavelic and supported by those determined to create their own state after what they saw as 20 years of Serbian dominance. The territory of the NDH covered almost the whole of today's Croatia and Bosnia and Hercegovina, but with considerable military and administrative restrictions in the part under Italian occupation. In May 1941, with the consent of the Pavelic government, Italy annexed a large part of mid and north Dalmatia plus some of the Adriatic islands and almost half of Gorski Kotar. With the approval and help of the Germans, the first Croatian military units were created consisting of 14 battalions of home guard (*Domobran*) and one regiment of extreme Croatian nationalists called Ustasha (derived from the Croatian word *ustanik*, meaning 'insurgent'). By the end of 1941 the NDH military forces consisted of 85,000 home guard, 16,000 Ustasha and about 6,000 people in the national police force. With full awareness of the nature of Serbian and Croatian antagonism, the Italians also created armed units drawn from the Serbian-populated areas in Croatia and made them part of their occupying forces. The Italians also helped the Chetniks in Bosnia and Hercegovina and coastal parts of Montenegro with arms and equipment.

In Serbia, the Germans created a puppet government led by Milan Acimovic. The police force was restored and three national police regiments were created, while in Belgrade a special police was formed to fight communism. In August 1941 a new Serbian government was formed under Milan Nedic who increased the size of the national police force to 10,000 men and created Serbian State Guard units numbering 5,000 people in total. A so-called 'Russian Protection Corps' of 2,000 people was created (consisting of Russian immigrants) to protect mines and other industrial plants.

Meanwhile, the Serbian colonel Draza Mihajlovic managed to reorganise the remnants of the shattered Yugoslav Army. Mihajlovic called his regulars Chetniks (the word *cheta* means 'bunch' or 'group')

The occupying forces protected the railways by building large brick bunkers reminiscent of medieval towers. This bunker was built to protect the bridge shown in the background and was manned by a crew of 10–15 men.

Two Chetniks photographed in 1943. Like the *Domobran*, many of the Partisans considered the Chetniks second rate adversaries. Unlike the *Domobran*, the Chetniks did not have a single type of uniform, nor did they have a unified military organisation.

from the name of the Serb nationalist organisation that had resisted Ottoman occupation, fought well in World War I, and had since existed as a reserve force to be called up when needed. The Yugoslav Royal Government-in-Exile in London appointed Mihajlovic as commander of the resistance forces within Yugoslavia, and then as Minister of Defence of the Royal Government-in-Exile. By the end of 1941 the Chetnik forces in Serbia had increased to about 20,000 strong.

In Slovenia, the Italians annexed half the territory, including the capital Ljubljana, imposed their language, and widely exploited the country, thus provoking armed rebellion. All civilian government was taken over by an Italian commissar.

The uprising begins

When it became clear that the capitulation of the Yugoslav Army was inevitable in April 1941, the KPJ started preparing for war and called on about 8,000 of its members to evade capture, gather together and stockpile weapons. In the years following World War II the KPJ declared that it alone had organised armed resistance but in fact a number of parties and independent anti-fascist groups had concealed weapons, waiting for an opportunity to fight. When Germany attacked the Soviet Union the KPJ considered this a favourable moment for an uprising. On 27 June 1941 the party's Politbureau founded the Supreme Headquarters of the National Liberation Army of Yugoslavia

Partisan guerrillas began by sabotaging railways, as shown in this photo. The vital line Zagreb–Belgrade was mined no fewer than 595 times. Explosives were mainly procured from unexploded bombs, artillery shells and field mines.

(*Narodnooslobodilacka vojska Jugoslavije* – NOVJ), and Josip Broz Tito was appointed its Commander-in-Chief. A proclamation was sent to all Yugoslav nationals urging them to join an armed uprising, and Partisan-style fighting (sabotage, raiding and hit-and-run missions) was adopted as the best method of resisting the occupying forces. Chosen representatives and clandestine groups were sent out from towns and cities with orders to create Partisan detachments.

In many of the remote villages, rarely visited by the occupying forces, armed groups were formed calling themselves 'peasant guard' or 'civil protection' units. Their role was to serve as protection from the armed remnants of the Yugoslav Army and other guerrilla and renegade groups that roamed the mountains. Both the occupation governments and the Partisans tried to win them over and make them part of their own forces.

It wasn't long before Partisan detachments started to fight the enemy all around Yugoslavia. By the end of 1941 the Partisans had some 80,000 fighters organised in a brigade, 49 detachments and 15 independent battalions. The following year the number of Partisans had increased to 150,000, and in January 1945 they numbered 800,000 organised in 52 divisions, 222 brigades and numerous individual detachments. During World War II some 300,000 Partisans were killed and 425,000 wounded.

Partisans with one of the first captured tanks in the mountain village of Audici at the end of 1942. Such events raised the morale of the Partisans and increased their respect among local villagers.

CHRONOLOGY

6 April 1941	Germany attacks Yugoslavia.
10 April 1941	The Independent State of Croatia (NDH) is proclaimed.
17 April 1941	The Yugoslav Army capitulates.
22 June 1941	Germany attacks the Soviet Union.
27 June 1941	The Politbureau of the Central Committee of the KPJ establishes the headquarters of the National Liberation Army of Yugoslavia with Josip Broz Tito as commander-in-chief.
4 July 1941	The decision to begin an armed uprising is taken at NOVJ headquarters.
August–September 1941	Partisans liberate about three-quarters of the territory of Serbia and Tito moves the headquarters to Uzice.
26 September 1941	Tito's headquarters are renamed the Supreme Headquarters (*Vrhovni stab* – VH).
October–December 1941	German units attack liberated territory in Serbia. This is known as the 'First Offensive' of the seven that occurred during the war.
January–February 1942	The 'Second Offensive' against the Partisans in Eastern Bosnia takes place.
March 1942	The 'Third Offensive' against Partisans in Eastern Bosnia, Hercegovina, and Montenegro is launched. All liberated territory is lost and the Partisans take heavy casualties.
24 April 1942	Partisan brigades begin an offensive in Eastern Bosnia. By early 1943 ten Bosnian towns have been liberated and a unified area centred on Bihac has been created of some 48,000 km^2 defended by about 30,000 Partisans.
20 January 1943	The 'Fourth Offensive' (a.k.a. the 'Weiss Offensive') begins, the largest to date. 90,000 soldiers attack the liberated territory around Bihac, Eastern Bosnia, which in German documents is referred to as 'Tito's territory'.
2 February 1943	The remnants of the German 6th Army at Stalingrad surrender.
9 February–13 March 1943	An important battle to save the wounded takes place on the River Neretva. The Supreme Headquarters, 15,000 Partisans and 4,000 wounded are surrounded. The Partisans manage to break out, but they suffer more than 50 per cent losses.
April 1943	British observers are sent to territory liberated by the Partisans.
12 May 1943	The Axis powers in North Africa capitulate.
May–June 1943	Continuation of the 'Fifth Offensive' in which 117,000 troops of the occupying forces attempt to wipe out the Partisan troops that have crossed the River Neretva in Montenegro. A second great battle to save the wounded takes place on the River Sutjeska.
10 July 1943	The Allies land in Sicily.
8 September 1943	The capitulation of Italy.
December 1943	Fear of an Allied landing in the Balkans provokes powerful attacks on the Partisan troops in Eastern Bosnia, Hercegovina and central Croatia: this action is known as the 'Sixth Offensive'.
25 May 1944	Axis forces carry out an airborne operation in Drvar, the 'Seventh Offensive'. The Germans do not manage to capture Tito, who escapes and is taken in an Allied plane to the island of Vis which becomes the main Partisan base.
6 June 1944	Allied forces land in Normandy.
12–13 August 1944	Meeting of Tito and Churchill in Italy. The Allies

	recognise Tito and the new Partisan governmental bodies in Yugoslavia.
9 September 1944	Units of the Red Army reach the Yugoslav–Bulgarian border.
20 October 1944	The liberation of Belgrade.
1 January 1945	Three Partisan armies are formed out of existing corps and divisions.
1 March 1945	The National Liberation Army of Yugoslavia, which has about 800,000 under arms, is renamed the Yugoslav Army.
20 March 1945	Beginning of the final operations for the liberation of Yugoslavia.
8 May 1945	The surrender of Germany.
15 May 1945	The last remaining enemy troops in Yugoslavia lay down their arms.

RECRUITING

In the summer of 1941, when the vision of a free country was distant and vague, people in various parts of Yugoslavia took up arms and joined the Partisans for a variety of reasons, not least a natural resistance to foreign occupation. In Serbia, the Germans had defeated their army, bombed their capital Belgrade, imposed high war damages and started a systematic plundering of goods. The rebellion in Uzice in 1941 was an indicator of the unrest this had caused. In the quisling NDH the Serbs were considered second-rate citizens and joined the Partisans or Chetniks on a massive scale, because of their fear of the extreme nationalist Croatian Ustasha.

The first Partisans

After the defeat of what is known as the April War, which led to the occupation of Yugoslavia, various mainstream pre-war political parties found themselves in uncharted waters. Attempts to organise armed opposition were mainly of a local character and based on the initiative of members of various pre-war, workers' or social organisations: this was particularly the case in Slovenia where the urban population was prominent and advanced. The Communist Party of Yugoslavia, on the other hand, was used to illegal operations and was able to continue with its political work through a well-developed conspiratorial network. Communists and those who sympathised with them had for some time been active among peasants, workers, students and those generally referred to as 'the progressive elements' of society in order to achieve their political aims. Also, the Communist Party was the only organisation active across the whole territory of Yugoslavia.

The way the KPJ organised the Partisan resistance units on Mount Kopaonik in southern Serbia provides a typical example of how it was done in many parts of the country. At the beginning of July 1941 the Party ordered their local committee in Kosova province and the town committee of Kosovska Mitrovica to form Partisan units on Mount Kopaonik. Kopaonik is the highest and most extensive

The youngest Partisans were the couriers. Poor radio contact made it necessary to use couriers – mainly teenage boys – to carry orders and messages. Many of them became famous for being able to carry messages across the most difficult and demanding terrain and in all weather conditions, bravely making their way through enemy lines to find the units they were looking for. Many of them lost their lives doing so too. Each of them had orders to swallow the paper on which their message was written in the event that they were captured or wounded or faced death.

13

A small parade of new recruits after a village in Slavonia has been taken.

mountain range in Serbia, covered by dense forests, and is 75km long and some 40km wide at its maximum extent. These members of the committee went to the mountains where, not far from the village of Lisin, they found a good site to set up a camp. Their choice of site was influenced by the terrain and the surrounding villages, whose inhabitants were sympathetic to their cause. With the help of local peasants they constructed a reception camp and supplied it with food and other requisites. They organised the collection of weapons and other military goods in the nearby Ibar valley, which the Yugoslav Army had abandoned after its defeat, and the local peasants concealed the cache before the German Army arrived. One heavy machine gun, four light machine guns, 55 rifles, three pistols, about 100 hand grenades and five boxes of ammunition were collected.

Under communist organisation seven miners created a diversion in the Trepca mines and then left for the camp. The committee then transferred another 12 miners from Trepca to the camp. The village schoolmaster from the Ibar valley brought in 20 Partisans in a group consisting of former Yugoslav Army soldiers, woodcutters, several village youths and one miner. An electrician arrived from Kosovska Mitrovica bringing seven secondary schoolboys with him, and so on. In early August 1941 in a single week 60 Partisans arrived: it is interesting to note that only six were communists.

In the region around the town of Tuzla and in Eastern Bosnia the situation was different. The regional Party committee for Bosnia formed a military committee for the Tuzla region with orders to organise an uprising. The Party branches in Maglaj, Doboj and Gracanica were ordered to collect information about people who were likely candidates for action. These were not to include extremists, nationalists or those who openly supported the occupation regime. Information was also collected about the amount of arms available and the points where an attack on the occupation troops was likely to be most effective. The date of 16/17 August was decided on for the beginning of the uprising: the aim was to capture Maglaj, Doboj, Gracanica and several railway and police stations. Their arms consisted of one heavy machine gun, 700 military and hunting rifles, 12 boxes of hand grenades and three boxes of ammunition. To give the impression of a larger force the 800 armed Partisans were joined by local peasants who came armed with pitchforks, axes and sharpened sticks. There were about 1,000 of them in total formed into units of 100: only their leader had a gun. The uprising did not manage to take Doboj but it did take Maglaj and Gracanica and captured three light machine guns, 230 rifles, 200 hunting rifles (taken earlier from the local population) and 15 boxes of ammunition. The occupation troops soon counter-attacked though and took back everything they had lost. Revenge and terror followed in which many civilians were killed and houses burned. Some of the organisers of the uprising and accompanying men managed to withdraw to Mount Ozren where a Partisan unit was formed on 26 August. The Ozren Partisan detachment then comprised 800 men armed with three light machine guns and 600 rifles.

The Party organised an uprising in Montenegro by forming armed groups for selected targets. However, when the order came for the beginning of the uprising a large number of armed Montenegrins took part and their numbers increased daily to reach an estimated 15,000. This well-planned uprising soon became a revolution. The Italian garrison was overrun and confined to a narrow strip of the coast. The Italians lost 2,000 men and large amounts of weapons and equipment. The organisers of the uprising found themselves overwhelmed by a new and unexpected situation. The Italians counter-attacked, joined by the Chetniks, and retook the territory they had lost. About 20,000 people fell victim to the ensuing terror. Small dispersed groups managed to escape into the remote mountain areas and from these the first Partisan units were formed.

Calls for mass uprising supposed that the war would finish in a few months and only produced short-term results. The KPJ admitted that this was the result of a lack of experience, and that it had not succeeded. With the organisation of smaller units the KPJ could keep the direction in its hands and carry out its policy of creating a command structure and achieving a proper balance in the use of manpower.

The first brigades

Relying on its clandestine contacts and communication methods the Party began to expand its numbers by gathering new recruits from the towns. The (illegal) Party members in the towns and villages continually worked on the people to join the Partisans. In addition a lot of people joined on their own initiative for various personal reasons, most often because of the harsh treatment meted out by the occupying powers. It often happened that more people went to join the Partisans than could be provided with weapons. Whenever any place or region was liberated there was a large number of new recruits.

Until the summer of 1944 the recruiting of Partisans had mainly been on a voluntary basis. With the liberation of Belgrade, the extension of liberated territory, and the creation of governmental bodies, recruitment became compulsory for all able-bodied young men. When Partisans entered a village that had been liberated they immediately began to muster new recruits. This was the reason for the increase in their numbers in the last years of the war.

Thanks to the constant influx of new recruits and the existence of a considerable number of Partisan units, from the beginning of 1942 it was possible to form battalions and brigades.

Presenting the colours at a review of the founding of the 2nd Dalmatian Brigade, 3 October 1942. The brigade flag and two of the battalion flags are Croatian tricolours (red, white, blue), the two other battalion flags are Serbian tricolours (red, blue, white). In line with the communist belief in 'brotherhood and unity' volunteers of one nationality were often directed to brigades which had a majority of another nationality in order to produce a multi-ethnic unit.

One of the characteristics of the Partisan war in Yugoslavia was the great number of women who participated. It was not uncommon for 10–20 per cent of a unit to be female. Though they considered themselves to be equal to the other soldiers, the remaining soldiers spared them from physical labour. Partisans addressed each other as 'comrade'. Many soldiers left their families behind: frequently they were the only surviving members of their families. As such, the detachment was their second home, and the presence of women gave it a special atmosphere. The soldiers respected their female comrades and many of these women died in battle trying to treat the wounded and injured. According to the unwritten rule, amorous relationships were strictly forbidden between men and women, and considered a sign of weakness. If a relationship did develope, it had to be very discreet.

The following example is typical of what began to happen all over Yugoslavia. On 19 May 1942 the 5th Krajina Detachment received the following despatch from supreme headquarters:

> You should form as many mobile Partisan battalions and brigades as possible to take part in important operations. Such units should be formed from young, healthy and physically active men with battle experience, men totally devoted to the national liberation movement and ready to fight in any situation that may arise. These men should cease to live in their villages and move to army camps under military discipline. Appoint courageous officers with the ability to lead young people.

The reality of the situation was described by a Partisan from the same detachment:

> We were mustered in front of an officer with a list in his hand. He called out the names of a number of us and told us we had been selected to go on a long journey with him. He said anyone who did not feel themselves capable of the arduous journey and the hard fighting which would follow should drop out there and then. Nobody would hold it against him. It was then that we discovered that we were to join a newly formed battalion. We were also told that we should exchange our clothes and shoes with those who were not going in order to be fully prepared. Those who were staying behind gave us their best clothing including weapons.

A detachment of 350 men joined 2nd Krajina Brigade as a third battalion.

In other parts of the country, similar events took place. The Kordun area of Croatia is largely Serbian: here the 5th Kordun Brigade was formed consisting of 790 Serbs and only nine Croats. In Slovenia the Tone Tomsic Brigade comprised 400 men of whom 30 were not Slovene. In the 4th Montenegro Brigade of 1,080 men 70 per cent were Montenegrin, the rest being Serbs.

Members of the Ustasha Muslim Militia who in spring 1944 went over to the Partisans. Throughout the whole war the Partisans were tolerant of the large Muslim population within Yugoslavia. These militia originated in Bosnia as a result of Chetnic violence against the Muslims from various parties, including Chetniks and fascists. From the end of 1943 the shape of the war and who would win became clearer, and these troops began to join the Partisans.

As part of their propaganda for the idea of 'Brotherhood and Unity' the Supreme Headquarters decided that single-nationality brigades, especially those operating in areas of mixed ethnicity such as Bosnia and Hercegovina, should be filled by recruits of different ethnic identities. The 1st Proletarian Brigade was composed mainly of Serbs but because of its military and political importance the Supreme HQ ordered on 13 January 1942 that it must include 300 Croatian Partisans. In the course of the war the 1st Proletarian Brigade listed 1,455 Partisans from Croatia, 1,515 from Bosnia and about 6,000 from Serbia or regions where Serbs were the majority population. Interestingly after the capitulation of Italy 120 Italians joined the Brigade.

Two Partisans photographed in early spring 1943. The one on the left has a German cap with an ordinary red star sewn onto it while the one on the right, judging by the hammer and sickle in the middle of the star, is probably a political commissar or member of a Proletarian Brigade.

Communist Partisans

On the day it was founded the 5th Kordun Brigade had 87 members of the Communist Party of Yugoslavia, 15 Party candidates, 60 from Party youth organisations (SKOJ): altogether communists made up 22 per cent of its strength. In 1942 the usual percentage was 30–50 per cent except in Slovenia where it was lower. The highest status which a brigade could attain was the elite title of 'Proletarian Brigade' which was achieved through proving itself in combat. During the war 14 brigades attained this status. The best fighters gained the title of 'Proletarian'. Because of selection of the best fighters for the Proletarian Brigades the percentage of party members in them was unusually high, sometimes over 60 per cent. For this reason even during the war Slovenian politicians accused the KPJ of forming their own Partisan army.

Organisation

The first Partisan military units were local companies and detachments. Each company usually had between 20 and 100 fighters, and each detachment had between 50 and 500 Partisans: some detachments had almost 1,000 men though. Larger detachments were composed of a number of companies. The smallest unit was a rifle squad of five to ten Partisans. Two to four squads formed a rifle platoon: there were two to four platoons in a company, and two to four companies in a detachment. The first battalions formed were little different to the detachments. The first real army formations were the brigades, conceived

A political commissar with the youngest member of the battalion – a 12-year-old courier. The commissar is wearing the parade uniform of a cavalry officer captured from a high-ranking *Domobran* officer.

Review of a division in summer 1944. Most of the Partisans here are wearing new British uniforms.

of as a unit of 1,000 fighters. The basic organisation was as follows: HQ with an escort and support company, four battalions each with four companies, and each company with four platoons. In practice brigades had 300–1,500 Partisans, and comprised two to six battalions. A support company was formed only if heavier weapons such as mortars and guns were available. Several brigades formed a division, several divisions a corps and several corps an army. A certain number of independent companies, detachments and battalions was incorporated into the brigades, and a smaller number remained in occupied territory functioning more or less independently until the end of the war. It was not rare for independent units to be reorganised several times over either because of heavy losses or because they had become part of a larger formation.

The officer corps

The German policy was to imprison officers of defeated armies. Most of the Yugoslav officers were imprisoned in Germany or joined the Chetniks. Later, through treaties with the quisling governments, a number of officers were permitted to return home on the condition that they serve in the armed forces of such bodies. The majority of the officers in the pre-war Yugoslav Army, particularly the high-ranking ones, were Serbs. The king had ordered the formation of the Chetniks, so the Serbian officers loyal to him who had avoided imprisonment, felt it their duty to serve in these units. Similarly, a significant number of Croat officers from the Yugoslav Army served in the Home Guard units. In both cases, the officers kept their ranks or were promoted to higher ones, in addition to receiving a wage for their service. Very few officers joined the Partisans, and gave up the security of the service and their privileges.

Since there were very few militarily educated officers in the Partisans, officers were chiefly selected from the ranks. In the process of selection and promotion to officer priority was given to the longest-serving members of the Communist Party (as individuals of trust), those who had previous military experience or were reserve officers or veterans from the Spanish Civil War, former police officers, and individuals of authority in their own region. Through personal excellence, bravery, combat experience and proven leadership ability, every Partisan could gain the respect of his fellow soldiers – and the Communist Party was keen to appoint officers who would be respected and obeyed by others. Once the command structure was established, officers in the units were recommended for promotion to high command, which they would generally accept. Promotions were also proposed and freely discussed at the Party meetings. As the war moved towards its end, the political demands on officership became increasingly complicated and similar to the Soviet model, in which allegiance to the homeland and to the Party was closely considered. Promotions at this stage depended greatly on the assessments given by political commissaries and members of the Party.

TRAINING

In pre-war Yugoslavia all males did a period of national service, so a certain number of Partisans had already received basic military training. However it was a characteristic of the guerrilla war in Yugoslavia that a large number of young men who joined the Partisans had no military experience. For example, when the uprising began in the Ozren mountains in summer 1941, of 2,000 men the only one with any military service was a retired sergeant. Another example is provided by the 1st Majevica Brigade: when it was founded at the beginning of 1943 it consisted of 960 Partisans of whom about 600 were between 17 and 19. Among the fighters of the brigade there were also 73 women. In the early years many who joined the Partisans found themselves immediately involved in the fighting. A recruit was teamed with an experienced fighter who would teach him some of the elements of Partisan warfare whilst in camp or in transit. Any further lessons would be self-taught through personal experience. Partisan Dragoslav Mutapovic from the 2nd Krajina Brigade wrote:

> It was mostly young people who joined us without experience and never having done military service. It was essential to teach them how to use a gun so that they could shoot at the enemy as well as they could. It was equally important to teach them how to avoid enemy fire. They trained in squads, troops and companies either during temporary lulls or before they went into battle. It was the custom to analyse every action after it was over and see what could be learned from it, considering the pros and cons. This was useful for both ordinary fighters and officers.

Some units had a well-thought-out training programme. One Partisan from the Kopaonik unit wrote:

Training courses, like the one shown here, were organised for education and information.

> In September 1941 the Partisan camp in Stanulovic village provided miltary and political training for its combat role. Teaching was done by reserve officers and NCOs. All kinds of specific training were organised, especially for young recruits, such as how to conduct ambushes, scouting, combat skills, military discipline and living, the use of explosives.

After the completion of the 'Fourth' (a.k.a. 'Weiss') offensive at the end of February 1943, the 15th

Learning how to use a British Boyce 13.97mm anti-tank gun, called 'John Bull' by the Partisans. They found this gun to be their best weapon against armoured trains. For example, on the night of 28/29 August 1944 two Partisans on the Mostar–Sarajevo line with 35 rounds put the engine of an armoured train out of action allowing their brigade to cross the line in safety.

Kordun Brigade held an advisory meeting with the officers of the brigade at the village of Nebljus. They discussed the problems experienced during combat and on the marches, and the new tactics the Germans were using in battle. It was concluded that the issues were the result of poor training, the lack of experience, and underestimating the German forces. It was decided to implement a training programme straight away for both officers and the troops. Over a period of 15 days, the troops were intensively trained in shooting with rifles, sub-machine guns and light machine guns and combat techniques. Unit-level training comprised squad, platoon and company in attack and defence, and company and battalion in defence in wooded terrain. The officers were taught the basic skills of map reading and communication between units during combat, and reconnaissance and scouting. Over 90 per cent of this training took place in the field.

Several hundred veterans from the Spanish Civil War joined the Partisans and provided valuable instruction on the organisation of fighting units and headquarters. Their knowledge often came to the fore in combat too, as seen in this quote on the attack on Bosanska Krupa on 18 June 1942: 'a civil war veteran showed us where to place the machine guns, how to move from one shelter to another and how to draw the enemy out so that we could attack him with hand grenades'.

Following the capitulation of Italy in 1943, a large number of Italians joined the Partisans – so many that they were formed into 19 brigades. They brought with them a wealth of military expertise which they shared with the Partisans. From 1944 the island of Vis became a large Partisan military base with a number of British commando and naval units based there. The British provided NCOs to help train the Partisans especially in gunnery and naval weapons. They also sent experienced personnel to train the Partisans in how to use equipment and weaponry, and in how to improve medical skills.

From the beginning of 1944 the Partisans went to British military camps in Italy and Africa for equipment and weapons training. Partisan officers also were sent to the Soviet Union where they attended officer training school with strict Soviet military and political drill. Many of the high-ranking Partisan officers completed their education at Soviet military schools and academies. The Soviet influence soon became apparent: from the end of 1944, as the communists took control of the liberated areas, so-called 'political training' became increasingly important alongside military training. A recruit in the 16th Vojvodina Division described this:

> New recruits are organised in separate platoons and companies which are part of battalions. Before going into active service they have ten days' military training. In addition the battalion commander together with the political commissar educate them, according to a set programme, in such subjects as the development and goals of the National Liberation Army of Yugoslavia; Comrade Tito as the leader of our people and other outstanding personalities of our uprising; servants of the occupier of our country, and seven other similar themes.

APPEARANCE AND EQUIPMENT

Uniform and dress

The first Partisan groups looked more like farmers, woodworkers and mountaineers than soldiers. Many men joined up in civilian clothing which was not suitable for prolonged outdoor wear: some even went in wearing their Sunday-best dress. At this time, uniforms of the ex-Yugoslav Army were also common, and the fighters often combined these uniforms with other clothing. Headwear was no less varied: traditional ethnic caps, hats, sporting caps, berets, fur hats and even antiquated Yugoslav military helmets could be seen. Individual fighters of the Kocevje Battalion continued wearing these helmets up until the summer of 1942. In September 1941, a decree by the Supreme Head-quarters ordered all Partisans in Yugoslavia to wear an anti-fascist red star on their caps.

In early 1942, the Croatian Partisans in the western part of Yugoslavia began wearing a new cap, called the 'Triglav cap', fashioned after a model some fighters had brought back from the Spanish Civil War. The Partisans in Slovenia, Dalmatia and western Bosnia quickly adopted this cap from their Croatian counterparts. From the end of 1942, Partisans in Eastern Bosnia and Montenegro began wearing caps similar to those of the Soviet Army. This cap, which was in fact Tito's idea, was named after him – the 'Tito cap'. The Tito cap began to replace the earlier Triglav cap, particularly following a decree passed in April 1944. The Partisans of the Gorenjsko region were particularly fond of their original caps, and many soldiers continued wearing them

The Partisans wore a great variety of uniforms. The one third from the left is wearing officer's riding trousers.

One of the early Partisans proudly posing in front of the camera in summer 1941. On his cap he is wearing a large five-pointed star made of red material. After their first battles and their first winter the Partisans quickly realised that they needed proper uniform and boots.

until the end of the war. In the 'France Presern' Brigade, an order was passed to confiscate the fighters' hats and burn them, and replace them with the Tito caps.

In mid-July, 1941, the Supreme HQ issued regulations for the appearance and dress of the Partisans, though these were more recommendations than orders. Each recruit was to receive the outlined clothing, undergarments, footwear and a blanket. This was implemented in some regions, though in most it was not.

Footwear was a particular problem: moisture, snow and many long marches wore out shoes over and over again. For example, the 2nd Krajina Brigade marched some 8,000km in the course of the war. Many soldiers wore *opanci* (the national shoe made of leather and without a sole). The headquarters of the divisions including the 1st and 2nd Vojvodina brigades sought assistance for footwear from the Supreme Headquarters in late June 1943, as 60 per cent of the soldiers were barefoot. In the impoverished villages of Yugoslavia, the village children and youths would normally be barefoot all summer, so some Partisans were used to a lack of adequate footwear. However, the situation was much more difficult in the winter. In January 1943, half of the soldiers in the 5th Kordun Brigade were without shoes, and instead wrapped their feet in cloth. In the fighting against the *Domobran* units near Saborsko, some of the soldiers were transported in 20 village wagons in order to protect their feet, yet some still succumbed to frostbite and had toes amputated. Though the brigade had already existed for 18 months, only with the capture of Otocac in April 1943 and the seizure of 1,000 used uniforms and pairs of shoes were all the soldiers dressed in full for the first time. There were numerous cases in which individual brigades lost between 10 and 20 per cent of their soldiers due to the lack of appropriate footwear.

The Partisan army did not have a special supply service at its disposal, and thus it primarily depended on its own local capacity to find food, equipment and money – and as such, the art of improvisation became a typical Partisan quality. In liberated areas, the Partisans organised civil government and set up the so-called People's Liberation Committee. This committee collected clothing for the Partisans, ranging from civilian dress to railway and fire-fighting uniforms. Only in 1944 were uniforms first sewn in Partisan workshops from cloth received from the Allies. These uniforms were, for the most part, khaki in colour.

A significant supply source for clothing and footwear were enemy soldiers who had been killed or imprisoned. In June 1943, under Mount Vucevo, the 1st Majevica Brigade broke through the German 118th Jäger Division and took few prisoners. Partisan Slavko Miccanovic wrote: 'About 60 Germans were killed on the battlefield. The number of wounded, missing and those who fell into the ravines could not be determined. The looting was extensive. Some Partisans immediately put on their new clothes and shoes. Virtually the entire 3rd Battalion of the brigade was dressed in the uniforms of the 118th Division.' Any captured *Domobran* units in comparison were stripped to their underclothes and sent back to their bases. Cases were recorded in which, following capture, individual *Domobran* units immediately began undressing, without being ordered to do so, as many among them had already been captured several times and knew what awaited them. In November 1943, the Partisans took the city of Tuzla, where they captured a warehouse containing 32,000 uniforms and 10,000 pairs of shoes, which were used to dress several divisions. As of 1944, Allied aircraft began dropping aid packages: by the end of the war, the Partisans had received some 180,000 pairs of shoes from Allied warehouses located in Italy. In Dalmatia, entire brigades were dressed in khaki-coloured British uniforms. In March 1944, the 1st Dalmatia Brigade received the first issue of these: one of the soldiers wrote: 'The supply officer called us to come with him to the storage facility. When he opened the door, we didn't know where to look first. We had received completely new clothing: undergarments, socks, shoes, shirts, sweaters, overcoats and belts. As we dressed we could hardly believe it.' In the last month of the war, General Vlado Segrt of 29th Hercegovina Division wrote: 'Our army is relatively well dressed even though we do all wear … a medley of uniforms … German, Italian, *Domobran*, British and other uniforms [and] civilian clothing … From the way our army is dressed, one can see its origins and the way it was created.'

Insignia and rank

The Supreme Headquarters decreed ranks in December 1942 and these simply defined the posts and duties of the unit's officers. At first, there were only six ranks, denoted by red ribbons and stars worn on the sleeve. In the first half of 1943, the number of ranks was increased to 18 due to

A barefoot Partisan on guard in a forest hospital. Lack of shoes was a serious problem. For example in the hard fighting carried out by the 16th Vojvodina Division in the Majevic mountains in November 1943 about 100 Partisans were killed and 430 wounded: of these, 130 cases were due to a lack of appropriate footwear.

Tito with the principal members of the General Staff at the end of 1944, at the capture of Belgrade. From April 1944 new khaki uniforms were issued with rank insignia in gold on the sleeves and collars. The cut shows a Soviet influence.

the formation of divisions and corps. As of May 1943, 14 new ranks from corporal to general were decreed. However, their implementation began only in early 1944. The ranks were denoted by a combination of ribbons and six-pointed stars. The four ranks for non-commissioned officers were silver, while the officer's ranks were gold in colour. The rank markings were normally worn on both sleeves 10cm from the cuff. With the introduction of the new ranks, the Supreme Headquarters created insignia for services such as artillery, supply, motorised units, doctors, medics, and others.

Personal weapons

The first Partisans were most frequently armed with the ex-Yugoslav Army weapons, which had been abandoned by soldiers and which were in abundant supply. The most common weapon at the time of the uprising and in the winter of 1941/42 was the Yugoslav Mauser M24 rifle and its shortened version, the M24 CK carbine. Also common were the Belgian Mauser M24, the Polish Mauser M29 rifle and the Czech carbine v.24, which were purchased in the hundreds of thousands prior to the war. Many Austro-Hungarian Manlicher M95 rifles and French M1907/15F rifles were left over at the end of World War I and these were used too. Despite this there was still a lack of military weapons, and so the Partisans frequently used hunting and sporting rifles. In 1941, the Montenegrins attacked the Italians armed with weapons produced between the Ottoman Wars and World War I.

The Partisan units formed in regions where the Royal Yugoslav Army was disarmed at first found it easy to gather weapons. For example, in March 1941, the Doboj Communists collected two heavy machine guns and 300 rifles from the abandoned equipment and arms from various units of the 2nd Yugoslav Army and the Bosnian Division. A farmer from that region recalled that for weeks they came across great quantities of varying arms and munitions on village roads and fields. The farmers took the bayonets, as they could also be used as tools back home. When the Germans arrived in the region of Doboj, Usora and Bare, they seized some 150 railcars full of munitions and weapons. A portion of this was sent to the Eastern Front, while the Partisans succeeded in destroying the remainder.

In other areas, the beginnings were more humble. The first units possessed some light arms from the Yugoslav Army, while the majority had hunting and sporting rifles. These weapons were first used to attack the smaller paramilitary stations and enemy patrols. As the quantity of seized arms increased, larger units became targets. In the battles from July 1941 to the end of the year, the Kordun Partisans seized nine heavy machine guns, 45 light machine guns, 729 rifles, four mortars and over 100,000 rounds of ammunition and 500 hand grenades from the Ustasha and *Domobran* units. The Dalmatian Partisans were even more successful. In that period, they seized

This photo shows how varied Partisan weapons were. In the foreground there is the highly regarded German MG42 light machine gun and in the pile a British Sten sub-machine gun can be seen, probably dropped by parachute.

enough weapons from the Italians and Chetniks to arm 2,000 fighters. In the records of numerous units and brigades, the information on weapons and munitions seizures is minutely detailed. It is interesting that bayonets are rarely mentioned, though they were also seized in large numbers.

As of the spring of 1944, the Allies gave substantial assistance to the Partisans in Yugoslavia and a large assortment of weapons was sent. One particularly detailed record shows this, as the origins and types of weapon are carefully documented. In April 1944, the 13th Hercegovina Brigade consisted of 1,304 Partisans, who were armed with 12 Breda M37mm heavy machine guns, 87 light machine guns (31 German MG34 and MG42, 20 Czech ZB vz.26 and vz.30, 19 Italian Breda M30 and 17 English Bren Guns), 27 sub-machine guns (11 German MP38 and MP40, ten English Sten, five Soviet PPSh-41 and one Czech ZK383), 918 rifles (679 Yugoslav and German, 193 Italian, 32 English, and 14 German rifles with anti-tank grenade launchers), four British anti-tank Boys rifles, and 15 mortars (seven Italian 45/5 M35, four German s.Gr.W.34, and four British M.L. 3in.). The brigade was equipped with 44,500 rounds of ammunition, 793 mortar grenades and only 30 hand grenades. In addition, the brigade also had 244 pack horses and mules, 15 draft horses to pull wagons and 22 riding horses.

Personal equipment

The Partisans frequently took items of personal equipment from enemy prisoners, such as leather belts and straps, ammunition pouches, pistol holders, bread bags, shelter-halves, entrenching tools, mess tins, and eating utensils, among others. Backpacks and large bags were most frequently used by the commissary and supply services. Binoculars, compasses and wristwatches were of particular value. The Partisan way of fighting was based on mobility and the ability to march long distances, which is why they avoided carrying a lot of equipment. In a war in which virtually everything was taken from the enemy, it was an unwritten rule that the Partisans could keep the seized weapons and equipment for themselves. If someone seized more than they needed, he kept what he required and gave the rest to the other soldiers. Only binoculars, compasses and map cases were given to the officers. One of the motives of battle in the front ranks was to capture the best weapons, uniforms, footwear or equipment.

A rare photograph taken from the rear showing the mixed nature of Partisan clothing and footwear, and how muddy they became.

A Partisan in Italian uniform with an officer's pistol.

CONDITIONS OF SERVICE

Daily life

The occupying forces concentrated their troops in larger towns and at economically important buildings, such as mines and factories. Patrols constantly monitored important communication routes, while every train station or key bridge held troops in bunkers, surrounded by barbed wire fencing. The Partisans were left to roam the forests and mountains, where they had their bases and shelters. The bases most frequently consisted of several quickly built wooden shacks in which the Partisans could secure temporary shelter and storage for munitions, food and medical supplies. Several such bases would often be built to provide extra security. However, sleeping quarters and long-term living quarters, particularly in winter, were possible only in certain villages where the inhabitants supported the Partisans. For the villagers, it was a great risk to take them in, as the enemy could retaliate by torching the village and forcing the inhabitants to flee deep into the woods together with the Partisans. For those deciding to stay in the village, death was the only result. Knowing this, the Partisans resolutely fought for and defended the villages for as long as they could. Their presence in one village meant protection from the local Ustasha, Chetnik or Muslim village militias, which were known to loot unprotected villages and kill the inhabitants. The largest villages had several hundred houses and were able to put up Partisan units of 100–200 men for longer periods of time.

The organisation and daily life of the Partisans in a village was typically as follows. The Partisans would select one house to be the headquarters of the detachment. In general, the staff would consist of the detachment commander, the political commissary, several men in the detachment on party assignment or as liaisons with higher staffs and smaller Partisan organisations in nearby towns, plus several Partisans in administrative roles. A well-equipped staff headquarters generally had a typewriter and several maps at its disposal. The staff also had several couriers, most frequently young men or boys who knew the terrain well and who were responsible for delivering orders and mail. Within the staff, a platoon of some ten armed men were always in position and on alert. The unit's guard, consisting of a platoon or entire company, was positioned in or around one of the houses. The sentries held their positions for several hours, although in winter months they replaced each other more frequently. Sentry positions were located at the edges of the village. Especially at night, the sentries were aided by village dogs. On the roads and paths approaching the village, an outpost sentry of three soldiers was positioned. One of these soldiers was responsible for transmitting urgent information to the staff. During the day and night, the Partisan patrols did the rounds of 'their' territory. If one of the

Mountain huts, usually a single room in which people worked, and slept.

soldiers was without footwear, another soldier would lend him his shoes for the duration of his guard duty.

The cook, his helpers of several local women and the soldiers responsible for horse transport, collecting firewood and physical labour were in another house. Three meals a day were cooked and, weather permitting, the soldiers would eat outside in the yard. The centre of daily life for the detachments was when the opportunity arose for the majority of soldiers to gather together in one place and to relax from their daily chores. The fourth most significant house was the medical service. If the detachment was lucky, it had a medical technician to assist the several female Partisans and village women. For these medical workers, the most difficult part was washing used bandages and dressings: throwing them away would be a waste, and thus these were often used several times. Due to a lack of medication, 'traditional medicine' was widely relied on.

The Partisans were particularly interested in forest sawmills and mines which had various tools and machines for working metal. They organised their first workshops for repairing and maintaining weapons.

A typical day in the village began with the Partisans gathering at dawn to be read the daily orders and duties. Those spared from duties could take the time to maintain their weapons or look after themselves. The recruits in the detachment had organised training, while the senior soldiers attended classes. These classes usually took place in a group of ten to 20 people. Officer, medical, radio-telegraph, and many similar courses were organised.

A political commissary was a person who 'had to know the political situation at every moment' and inform the soldiers of such. He was also the president of the communist alliance within the detachment. He called the meetings and was responsible for political activity. At these meetings, the Partisans would be free to criticise themselves and others, pointing out mistakes or improper behaviour. One example of such criticism might be that directed at a female colleague who had put on lipstick, thus 'corrupting' the youth in the village.

The detachment also received news via bill posters put up on a dedicated wall. They could read about the events in the world, and the stories of soldiers who had been exemplary in some way. The village dwellers would easily fit in with the daily life of the soldiers, and vice versa. The Partisans helped the villagers in their daily tasks and were often welcome on village farms, as the majority of the soldiers themselves were farmers who knew how to work with livestock and crops. Several soldiers slept in every house. Women soldiers slept in separate quarters.

Opportunities for entertainment in the village were rare. They were most frequently organised by the younger members of the detachment. The political commissaries organised public gatherings at which both the people and the Partisans could explain the goals of the liberation war and so on. Following this, an outdoor dance would take place.

A Partisan hospital hidden deep in the forest. Such hospitals were usually no more than several wooden barracks and could accommodate about 100 wounded. Usually an underground shelter was dug near the hospital where the wounded and hospital personnel could take refuge in an attack. In the famous battle to rescue wounded between the Sutjeska and Neretva rivers in 1943 the enemy found 700 wounded and hospital personnel in underground shelters at Trnava, Bukovac and Jakov and killed them all.

Such quiet and idyllic periods could not be taken for granted. Prior to an enemy offensive against them, the villagers would flee into the woods and the Partisans would protect them as much as they were able to. Once an offensive had passed through, only ruins remained. These would be hard times for all. In order for the detachment to survive, they had to find another village to take them in, or they would welcome another brigade into their formation as reinforcement. The life of soldiers in the brigades was significantly different. Frequent moving and combat was substantially harder to bear, and as a result, the losses were higher. Exhausted brigades would be given the chance to spend a longer period of time in one place, to rest and recharge. Due to the large number of fighters, they were put up in several villages. Many wounded and exhausted soldiers requiring rest were put together with those preparing and ready for battle.

Food

The basic sources of food for the Partisans were contributions from local peasants, war booty, requisition, confiscation of the property of collaborators, and Allied aid. In this guerrilla war it was not possible to build up or carrry large supplies so the main source was the local population who, being in considerable need themselves, provided only basic foodstuffs.

Women carrying food to the Partisans on their heads, a typical method at this time in Yugoslav villages. Such food from the local people was essential. Knowing this the enemy often burned villages which they suspected of helping the Partisans.

In liberated territory, People's Committees were organised to collect food. In so doing they took great care to collect equally from various people, something the peasants were equally careful to keep an eye on. In Partisan villages the committees kept a list of contributing households and allocated what each should give. If there was nothing for the villagers there was nothing for the Partisans. If the Partisans managed to capture larger quantities then they shared it with the peasants. Winter was the most difficult time, together with periods during enemy offensives which could last as long as two months. In the latter case

the Partisans might be forced out of the liberated areas to take refuge in the mountains. The situation was not always bad especially if the Partisans managed to hold on to liberated territory for a considerable period. In autumn 1943, one quartermaster managed to provide for the village of Sehovici from the Srijem harvest 240 tons of wheat, 20 tons of potatoes, four tons of beans, 880 tons of bacon, 420 tons of onions and one mobile mill. Other important sources of supplies were successful ambushes and captured enemy warehouses.

One way of solving the problems of food supply: the pig farm of the 6th Corps deep in the woods in the winter of 1943/44.

From 1944 onwards the Allies parachuted large amounts of food to the Partisans and brought food by air to secret airstrips. The Partisans had their first taste of powdered food at this point: either because they did not know what to do with it or did not have time, they first ate the powder and then drank water, provoking some confusion and hilarity.

Discipline

Discipline in the detachment was never as strict as in battle brigades, particularly in the Proletarian Brigades. While a soldier sitting down on guard duty could be tolerated in the detachment, in the brigade the soldiers stood on guard as outlined in all regulations of military service. In the detachment, the ritual of the military salute and correct communication between an officer and soldier was reduced to a minimum level of observance. There was no expectation for the barefoot Partisan, or one wearing light sandals, to stamp his heels or to march in strict military step. Salutes were made with a clenched fist. It was not rare for a Partisan to salute an officer while officially submitting a report, and then for the two men to embrace each other in a friendly manner. Many set off together for war and were brothers in arms from the very beginning of service. Off duty, the relationship between officers and Partisans was friendly, they ate and joked together, although authority was never questioned. By the end of the war the Partisans began to resemble a more typical army. However, relationships between the hierarchy and veterans continued to be less formal, while with new recruits it was truly military.

Disciplinary violations were ruled on by head-quarters, court martial or the local KPJ organisations. If the local party organisation thought there were mitigating circumstances in the offender's favour, then the punishment was less severe – or alternatively it could be stiffened if the opposite was the case. One of the most serious violations a soldier could commit was to take something without permission from a farmer, a sympathiser or someone offering shelter to Partisans. A respectful attitude towards civilians was vigorously enforced. One Partisan was shot dead in front of his comrades because he took a woollen shawl without asking from a woman's house in winter 1942.

BELIEF AND BELONGING

The Partisan's war (or as the communists called it, the National Liberation War) was a combination of international warfare, a struggle against occupation and a socialist revolution – a key difference to other European guerrilla movements in World War II. The communists successfully managed to bring various factions together, reconcile differences and steer them in a single direction, which they defined as the struggle against 'the occupier, his servants and national traitors'. They accorded all people equal status regardless of ethnic identity, race or religion, and promised free elections after the war ended, in which people would be able to decide what kind of country they wanted. During the war, as the Partisan movement grew stronger, a diversification of opinion developed over the latter point, with a moderate civic option at one end and the extreme communists at the other.

Two Partisans showing the characteristic clenched fist salute introduced by the Yugoslav communists from the Spanish Civil War. In the background is a young olive tree showing that the photograph must have been taken not far from the Adriatic coast.

Having liberated an area, the Partisans seized great expanses of land, factories and property. According to the communist ideal, capitalists were the enemy of the workers and farmers, and were allied to the occupying powers. A very small number of capitalists supported the Partisans, and their property was not touched during the war. Only after the end of the war would capitalist and church property be nationalised virtually in its entirety. The explanation behind this act was very simple – the 'People's Government' had handed the people what belonged to the people. For the typical soldier, a new time had come in which things would be better for all following victory. Everything belonged to the people, meaning it belonged to him. This was the essence of the socialist revolution and one of the key motives which kept the Partisans moving forward. They fought not only for freedom, but also for social reforms after the war. Farmers would receive land and workers would manage the factories.

The war in Yugoslavia was exceptionally brutal, particularly for the civilian population which suffered greatly in certain regions. Entire villages were destroyed if they belonged to a different ethnic group or if they supported the Partisans. The winter cold, hunger and illness all took their toll. For the Partisans, these were other evils to fight against, which only motivated them further. The Germans considered the Partisans to be bandits who deserved merciless extermination. Captured Partisans could expect certain death and, knowing this, they often fought to the bitter end.

During the war, the KPJ created the ideal of the communist fighter, which every Partisan was to aim towards. Above all, he was to be brave and resolute, always in the front line and an example to everyone; humble and willing to share his troubles with others; willing to encourage his fellow soldiers in the most trying of situations; and able to accept criticism from others and to point out others' mistakes. At the time, this was a positive concept which motivated a great number of soldiers, particularly the younger ones. After the war, a change of direction took place in this regard, similar to the Soviet model. However, the fact remains that during the war a great number of communists died in battle hailing freedom, Tito or the party at the very moment of their deaths. In the last year of the war, when a large number of new recruits was mobilised, the dedication and enthusiasm of the earlier years was not so evident.

A Partisan kitchen in a beech forest in late autumn. The Partisans had great difficulty in getting hold of salt and often had to serve unsalted food. In Eastern Bosnia prisoners of war were often exchanged for 50kg bags of salt.

Friendship and camaraderie were also part of the communist ideal. One of the greatest criticisms that could be levelled at a soldier would be to suggest that he was not acting as a comrade. Regardless of the ideology, among groups of people who live and fight together and who depend on each other, strong bonds of friendship and a real feeling of belonging to the group are formed. In these groups, the soldiers were fighting not only against the enemy, but also for each other. This kept morale levels high. Courage was particularly esteemed: as a result, the brave became even braver, and those less brave gave their best to follow behind as well as they could.

The Partisans had little opportunity to put on parade uniforms, show off medals or campaign badges, or to take part in parades. The political commissary of 2nd Dalmatian Brigade wrote when passing through a small Dalmatian town in 1944:

> After two days of battle, we were tired, dirty and hungry. Passing through a town, the people there ran out onto the streets to wave at and greet us. The battalion commander told one soldier with a strong voice to lead the troops in a song. They sang with him, loudly and clearly. We raised our heads, our exhaustion disappeared and each step became stronger and more resolute. The people watched us and admired us. They said, 'There goes the people's army, the Proletarians'.

Such events are often recalled in first-hand accounts, seen as a small but important reward for so much suffering and sacrifice. The pride of belonging to a unit and of being Partisans was common to them all.

ON CAMPAIGN

Living in the woods

Three-quarters of Yugoslavia's mountainous terrain was covered in dense forest at the time of World War II. Numerous Partisan units operated in these regions and some of the most difficult battles were

After the capitulation of Italy, the Partisans with the help of the local population took enormous quantities of ammunition and weapons into the woods. Members of the 13th Primorje Division alone took 500 heavy and light machine guns, 130 sub-machine guns, 15,000 rifles and 150 tons of ammunition to their base. Small oxen and low carts were the best transport vehicles in the mountainous regions of Yugoslavia.

fought here. The climate was harsh, with five months of snow and only three warmer summer months. When the Partisans were not in their bases in the settlements, they spent the majority of their time in the woods. The forest was considered their second home, with good reason. During the summer, life there was bearable. There were large quantities of firewood, and with the numerous springs, streams and mountain rivers, there was ample drinking water. The enemy avoided the forests and as such, the Partisan forces felt safe there. They did not stay in the same place for long and the woods provided an excellent operational base for raiding enemy towns and disrupting communications. Short-lived attempts to pursue the Partisans ended unsuccessfully, as the woods would swallow them up quickly.

Woodland camps were similar to mountain camps with one exception: the Partisans did not have tents, and the whole camp was set up in order to be able to move away quickly on command. The experiences of a Partisan cook Zivko Djokic of 2nd Krajina brigade provides typical details of this:

In mountain warfare horses were also considered an excellent means of transport and were used by both sides. In the most difficult periods they were also an emergency source of food.

> At night we had to find water and wood and get the fires going. We had to eat in complete silence and then continue the march, we cooks did not have a moment to rest. Sometimes we ate beans that had been cooked five times over: we would just finish cooking them and an attack would begin – by Chetniks, Ustasha or Germans – and we would douse the fire but somehow save the beans. When we stopped again we would put them in a new lot of water and cook them again. The order 'Fires out – Advance' often came several times.

Slovene Partisan, Liberation Front, 1942

A

B

Training to use the M15 gun, summer 1944

Weapons

1

2

3

4

5

6

7

8

9

V.Vuksic

C

D

A Partisan ambush

Living in the woods

E

Assault on an Italian pillbox

Mount Zelengora, June 1943

G

Machine gunners of the Vojvodina Brigade and Hercegovina Brigade, spring 1944

The Partisans usually slept on dry leaves or bare earth. Many learned to sleep sitting up, leaning on tree trunks. The routine life between battles saw guards in position, and patrols conducted in the surrounding area. In the mountain meadows, young Partisans led the horses to graze, while others cut firewood or fetched water. When the nights were cold the soldiers slept close to the fires. There was always one soldier responsible for keeping the fire burning all night long. Improvised shelters were put up quickly to protect the wounded, the headquarters, the radio if they had one, and food and munitions. Bad weather was a frequent occurrence in the mountains, with heavy rainfall and electrical storms. Such adversity had to be stoically faced. Any captured raincoats or shelter halves were given to the wounded, the sick, women and courier boys. In the damp forests, wet clothes took days to dry out.

Winter was an exceptionally difficult period. Knowing this, the enemy launched large-scale operations against them in the harshest conditions, pushing the Partisans into the forests and the hills. Compared to the well-equipped and well-dressed German mountain troops, the Partisans were poorly dressed and half-starved. Partisan Pero Gavric of 1st Proletarian Brigade provides a vivid picture:

> I don't know exactly how many rough days and sleepless nights we spent in the forests and mountains, but I think it was about 11 or 12. Finally, one day we came across a passage through a mountain meadow, where the snow was about half a metre deep. When we began climbing again on the other side, a soldier fell from his horse into the snow. He was frozen solid. After 100m or 150m, another fell. At the top of the climb, the order was passed through the column – to move forward as best we could. That meant that we were not to help any of the others.

Marching

The Partisan style of warfare required maximum mobility, which meant that marching was an everyday part of life, in all conditions. The fact that they did not have heavy weapons and equipment meant that they could move at short notice and could cover much more ground in a day or night than an ordinary unit. It was a regular occurrence for a brigade to cover 50km in a day or night and on long marches they averaged 30km a day and a further 20–30km at night. Small units were able to cover even greater distances. The 13th

On the roads Partisans usually marched in two files as shown here.

Hercegovina Brigade marched 63km in 20 hours in April 1945, through the forests of Mount Javorik, in the snow and rain, probably the longest march undertaken by any brigade. In the campaign to push into Serbia in the summer of 1944, the 16th Vojvodina Division marched 812km between 23 July and 3 September. The division's headquarters precisely recorded all the march distances in a journal, which described one part of the journey as follows: 5th July – 30km, 6th – 26km, night of the 6th/7th – 35km, day and night of the 7th – 45km, and so on. Such marching was not without cost: 67 soldiers died along the way from hunger and exhaustion.

Organising a march for a unit of any size was complicated and always open to risks of many kinds, which meant that it had to be well planned. The first stage was the arrival of the courier with orders from higher command. As soon as he arrived, the fighters knew that something was about to happen. The plans were discussed by the commanding officers or their deputies, and to preserve maximum security only they knew the route to be taken. Couriers were sent to other units involved and to Partisan sympathisers whose job was to organise the reception at destination. They also acted as guides: because marches were usually undertaken at night, information about the strength of the enemy and the positions of his sentries and patrols was essential. Passwords and recognition details were also decided on.

Preparations for the march were made by day: each Partisan was given ammunition and a bag of food for three days, mainly consisting of rough maize bread (inedible after a week) and full water bottles. Partisans who did not have ammunition pouches carried bullets in their pockets. The troops were mustered in one place, addressed by the commander and reminded of strict discipline. The commander and quarter-master had the most to do. Any supplies taken needed to be kept to a minimum. If the unit had a cannon or mortar then more horses would be needed to carry this. The main load was made up of ammunition, explosives, spare barrels for machine guns, wire and cords, axes, saws, shovels and similar tools. Because of the importance of the supplies each horse was led by a Partisan. The quartermaster knew a little more about the route than most fighters and how long the food supply had to last. Food, field kitchens and cooking equipment all had to be taken, and this was carried on several horses.

The marching order was decided in advance. First came the advance guard of several fighters, then the staff with the couriers and then the companies one after another. The quartermaster was at the rear: in enemy territory there was also a rear guard. A march would typically begin at dusk. In especially foggy or dark conditions the fighters

Along paths and in open country the Partisans would march in single file. This provided a smaller target for the enemy and meant they could take up battle positions very quickly. The drawback was that a brigade might be strung out over several kilometres. For this reason it might take a whole night for a brigade to cross a railway line that was well patrolled by the enemy.

A group of Partisans fast asleep after an exhausting night march. The photograph was taken in the final months of the war, when the Partisan troops were following directly behind the enemy. Such scenes were common.

Partisans turning their hands to cobbling in the forest between marches. Worn-out shoes were mended by using old car tyres.

would keep in voice contact starting from the head of the column, calling out and responding 'first', 'second', 'first', 'second' and so on. Every few hours a rest halt was called – and so it went on until morning. The routes were generally planned so that by breakfast the unit had reached a friendly village where it would rest. If roads or railway lines had to be crossed detachments would take up positions a few hundred metres either side of the crossing point, and would only leave when the whole column had crossed. Bridges were chiefly in enemy hands or had been blown up so rivers had to be crossed with boats or hastily assembled rafts, unless shallow enough to be waded. Mountain rivers and streams more than waist deep were especially dangerous and for that reason swimmers were placed beside non-swimmers and the rivers crossed holding hands in a long chain.

Winter marching for the poorly clothed Partisans was incredibly exhausting. Commander Todor Vujasinovic of Ozren detachment described what it was like forcing their way through deep snow: 'The detachment was moving towards Mount Konjuh, the snow was above our waist. Every 100 to 200 metres we changed the forward company that was making the path for the others.' One of the most arduous marches undertaken was that across the Igman mountains in Bosnia on the night of 25 January 1942: the temperature was –32°C and a snowstorm was raging. It took 18 hours for 730 fighters to cover 10km. One hundred and seventy of them suffered serious frostbite with 100 minor cases too. In the hospital at Foca many of them had to have amputations, without anaesthetic.

Preparing for combat

The preparations for combat began with field reconnaissance. Local residents, employees in the occupying government who sympathised with the Partisans, illegal communist groups in larger towns and in some cases escaped Chetnik and *Domobran* deserters provided confidential information to the Partisans. Prisoners were also a valuable source of information. Most often, the Partisans were interested in which unit or crew was in situ, how large it was, its positions, daily routines, morale and other such matters.

Attack was the principal form of combat activity. They were usually launched at night or just before dawn in order to avoid the attention of enemy aircraft, tanks and artillery. The soldiers approached the attack area in columns, before transferring to combat order, which was a complex process. Preparations for the attack began some 20km or more before the target. Surprise was one of the most powerful weapons the Partisans had, and as such, the entire operation revolved around it. The most difficult part was estimating the time the detachment would need to reach their combat positions in order to coordinate a simultaneous attack with other Partisan units. Arrival at the firing line had to be within minutes of an attack starting, and thus all preparations had to be completed well in advance. The difference between experienced and inexperienced units was telling in this regard. The Proletarian Brigades certainly led the way in this respect.

The battle preparations for the detachment began before the final approach march: if the detachment was already experienced in battle, then they began during the last, so-called 'attack phase' of the march. Prior to the attack, the soldiers ate very little, for if they were injured in the abdominal area that would increase their chances for survival. The soldiers were organised into assault and bomber (*bombasi*) groups, which were never larger than ten men. Each assault group had equipment to hand for overcoming barbed wire, obstacles and minefields. Most frequently, this consisted of wooden planks or an ordinary ladder, though they also carried cutters, axes, saws and any other tools which could be used. The bomber groups consisted of the bravest soldiers. The best among them would be organised into the first platoon of each company: the first platoon of the first company was the elite of the detachment or battalion. The bombers received their own fire christening when they were hit with shrapnel from their own bombs. Each bomber carried five to ten bombs, some attached to their belts, others in their pockets or in bread bags. To maintain stealth and mobility, they would carry only a pistol and bayonet. For this reason each bomber group was supported by several soldiers in a close support group to back up their attack with gunfire from the immediate vicinity. An attack column would typically consist of a bomber, assault and close support group. The final outcome of the battle for the inhabited town frequently depended upon the 'breakthrough group', who were tasked with tackling and destroying the enemy positions and preventing reoccupation. Unlike the bomber group, this group carried the main weapons and explosives. The best sub-machine gunners were in this group. Further support groups were also organised and one of the companies was set up as a reserve.

Several kilometres ahead of its target, the detachment would silently change formation from the marching column to several attack columns. Each column would have its commander, munitions and several female Partisans responsible for pulling out the wounded. Horses were left behind with the medical staff, so that they could be used to move the wounded. The unit was then ready to attack.

THE EXPERIENCE OF BATTLE

The attack begins

The village of Saborsko, which is located in the mountainous Lika region of Croatia near the Zagreb–Rijeka railway line, provides a good example of how the forces occupying Yugoslavia in early 1943 defended and fortified a village strongpoint and its surrounding area. In this well protected village there were 200 *Domobran* troops, 50 paramilitary policemen and 20 armed civilians. At the railway station of Licka Jasenica, only 3km from Saborsko, an infantry battalion of the Italian Re Division was stationed. There were 300 Chetniks in Licka Jasenica, while yet another Italian Re battalion division was in the village of Plaski. At Vrhovina there was a battalion of the Italian Macerata Division and a battery of 100mm howitzers of the Lombardia Division, with one company responsible for the protection of the railway line. In the villages of Blato, Plavac and Plaski, there were about 400 Chetniks. Altogether, there was a total of 3,000 troops standing by to assist any attacked town or village.

The occupying forces fortified Saborsko and many other places with the same strategy of three lines of defence. The outer line was made up of trenches and pillboxes, surrounded by barbed wire and minefields. The next line consisted of the stone buildings and concrete bunkers. The third and final line, the last stand, was in the main square of the village. This line was dominated by the largest building (a school, post office or municipal building) which was strongly reinforced: the headquarters were located there. Telephone and radio communications were used to contact other units. One or more artillery batteries provided fire for a radius of about 10km from the centre.

Two to three Partisan detachments, or an entire brigade, were required for an attack on a place like Saborsko, and if they took such a place, they could secure food and munitions for a considerable period, and some of the soldiers would receive weapons, clothing or footwear too. However, the Partisans were facing a better-armed and more numerous enemy that had tanks, artillery and aircraft at its disposal. Their chief weapon was the

The Partisans considered the *Domobran* (home guard) second-class opponents except for their one or two mountain brigades like the one in this photo. Most home guards surrendered without firing a shot or after a very short exchange. When the Partisans captured them they let them go home after they had taken their uniforms, shoes and weapons. Some home guards were captured several times: many opted to join the Partisans.

In the middle of 1944 the British equipped a Partisan brigade with 56 American M3A3 Stuart light tanks and 24 AEC Mk II armoured cars: a little later the Soviets equipped another brigade with 65 T-34/85 tanks. The photo shows M3A3 tanks ready for the beginning of the operation to take Knin in Croatia.

element of surprise, with a rapid and forceful attack: if the village was taken, they needed to quickly and systematically take everything they could and withdraw into the woods. In actions against larger enemy strongpoints where reinforcements might be sent in to assist the enemy, the Partisans set up ambushes and blockades tasked with holding back such reinforcements for as long as possible. A decisive factor in the success of an attack was ensuring it came from all sides and that these assaults all came at the same time. When it did take place, the attack came at night or early in the morning in order to avoid the attention of enemy planes. The Partisans also knew how to take advantage of fog, rain and other inclement weather conditions to achieve surprise.

The bomber team usually comprised younger soldiers who were fitter and able to overcome barriers and obstacles on the approach to target. The best among them were able to throw explosives into an enemy bunker 10m away in the dark, guided only by the flash of the firing enemy machine guns. They would launch their attacks only after they had managed to steal up to the bunker undetected. The attack on the *Domobran* concrete bunker in Gorenja Vas in December 1944 was described by the commander of the bombers team of the Vojkova Brigade:

> The snow was deep and the night was cold. We crawled to the bunker which was some 50m away. The snow crunched under our feet and we were afraid they could hear us. I took 10 grenades, and my soldiers took six each. The enemy fired shots into the air every now and then out of nerves. In the bunker ahead of us, I could hear their voices and could smell cigarette smoke. They still did not know we were there. One soldier, lying on his back, cut the wires and made a way through, and we crawled through after him. All of a sudden the bunker to the right of us was racked by explosions. We couldn't wait any longer and we ran the last ten metres. We threw our grenades into the bunker before they could fire a single bullet.

With the first explosions, the support group would open fire on the enemy positions while the assault groups would move to overcome the barriers and open the way for the remaining assault troops to move through to the inner defences. Very often, this phase achieved complete surprise, so that the Partisans easily overcame the outer defence line. The second line was more difficult as the enemy had gathered itself in the meantime and was ready to resist. This phase relied on the strength of numbers to penetrate the town or village itself. Bomber teams were also included in these groups, as they were effective weapons in the battle for the fortified buildings. Their task was to cut off the enemy and prevent reinforcements from arriving. If one of the detachments or battalions was late for some

Women and old men carrying wounded Partisans through a mountain village, winter 1942/43. Without the support of the local people, as in this extreme example, the Partisans would never have been able to achieve the success they did.

reason in executing their attack, the defence would be better organised in that sector with reinforcements sent to other endangered sections. The push to the centre of the town, which was also the central point of the defence, forced the units in the peripheral buildings to retreat in order to avoid being surrounded and destroyed. In a night attack, individual assault groups would set fire to outhouses and lesser buildings as they were taken so that the Partisan headquarters, watching the battle from afar, could see how far the attackers had got. The Partisans were then left with overcoming resistance in the centre of the town. If the enemy troops had low morale, they gave in very quickly: however, Germans and the Ustasha were the toughest to break. It was not uncommon for such units to hold out until reinforcements arrived from outside the town.

On average, one in three attacks ended in failure, or had only limited success. The most frequent causes of failure were the absence of a certain unit which was supposed to have participated in the attack, a poorly coordinated beginning, detection or pre-warning of the Partisans' presence, the arrival of reinforcements from the outside, or a lack of sufficient firepower. Partisan Ibrahim Meskovic of 17th East Bosnian Brigade wrote about a failed attack on the German trenches and bunkers near the village of Memici in December 1943:

> We were pounding the German bunkers with all our weapons. I had run out of ammunition for my machine gun since my assistant had got lost somewhere in the dark. Our company used the dark to try to break through to the German trenches. But there, the situation was terrible. Whoever tried to move forward was shot down. Whoever tried to pull out the dead or wounded was killed too.

Due to the short period of time available to prepare the attack and the lack of knowledge of minefield locations, some assault groups suffered extensive casualties. In the assault by soldiers of the 2nd Dalmatian Brigade on the town of Sujica in December 1942, 15 fighters were killed and 25 injured when they hit a minefield on their approach.

The wounded had to be carried on makeshift stretchers, usually two poles with a sheet stretched between them. The Partisans were often forced to withdraw carrying the wounded with them which not only slowed them down but made taking difficult routes out of the question. This meant they often had to use more risky routes.

The importance of attacking

The Partisan assaults on fortified towns were carried out exclusively using infantry forces, and they would be launched at full speed. The aim was to launch the main breakthrough attack (following the assault group's work) at a distance of less than 50m. Attacking became an almost instinctive procedure for the Partisans, as shown in this account:

We moved quietly in column. When we came within 30 metres of a wooded slope, suddenly the Germans opened up with machine guns. Fortunately, the bullets hit the snow some two metres ahead of us. Our commander, who always moved at the head of our column, jumped to the side and immediately ordered us to launch our attack. We were ready in a flash, and began the assault, shooting. The Germans were taken by surprise and they immediately retreated.

Attacking was not just used to take specific objectives or to overcome enemy positions: it was also used to break out of an enemy encirclement. Even in no-win situations, attack remained the only option: especially when ammunition was low or spent, it was the only way to inflict losses upon the enemy. The attacking enemy was allowed to approach as close as possible, and was then hit with grenades and all available firepower to create the maximum confusion. If and when the enemy retreated, a new attack would be prepared for, the wounded would be quickly pulled in, and the weapons and ammunition of the dead collected. The soldiers quickly retreated to their positions and awaited a new attack.

The Partisans' tactical aim was to create confusion and disorder. In the 'Fifth' offensive, the Germans advanced in four columns into the Sutejska river valley and began preparing for battle. Lacking the time to retreat or to take up better positions, two Partisan brigades moved to launch an assault against their superior opponent. The confusion which resulted was used to cover their successful retreat. These surprise assaults bewildered the Germans, whose reactions were frequently slow. The German tactics differed in the formations for attack and defence, and they required time to switch from one to the other. However, the Partisans had no such difference: how they attacked was how they defended.

Defensive measures

The Partisans sometimes found themselves having to prevent the enemy from moving into liberated territory or to protect civilians and the wounded. As a general rule, their 'local' enemies (such as Chetniks and *Domobran* units) were not the ones they feared most. One soldier of the 15th Majevica Brigade wrote disparagingly about a particular Chetnik attack on their positions:

They attacked senselessly and without any order. Our bomber went along the slope just above our position and greeted the Chetniks with bombs several times, returning them to their starting positions … There were several critical moments when we retreated. As night approached, the Chetnik attacks became weaker and less frequent. They suffered great losses.

However, in January 1943, the Partisans were for the first time faced with an attack by the crack German mountain-troop unit, the

In 1944, thanks to Allied help, the number of radios and transmitters increased. However, the lack of a unified coding system and the fact that some of the enemy spoke the same language meant the Partisan radio operators had to invent their own recognition signs. In spite of this the enemy often managed to infiltrate their radio communication systems.

7th SS 'Prinz Eugen' Division. The Germans applied new and surprise tactics against the Partisans. They attacked in several columns, each of which was so strong that the Partisan units could put up no serious resistance. They moved in linear formations, and in some places, small columns would separate from the main ones moving around the Partisan position, and during the night they would sneak up on their rear. This tactical change confused the Partisan soldiers and officers, who up to that point had never come across this strategy. The German commander quickly spotted the Partisan weak points: a lack of ammunition, their habit of firing too early, poor communications, and too little attention given to scouting, monitoring and maintaining contact with the enemy. The Germans quickly and effectively took advantage of these weaknesses in their aggressive approach. In January 1943, during the 'Weiss' offensive, the Germans used this strategy to sneak up behind a brigade and to surround one of its battalions with some 150 soldiers. A section of the battalion succeeded in breaking through the enemy encirclement, and one soldier, Mico Uzelac, has left a vivid account of events:

The explosions, the screams of the wounded and dying, the shouted orders from the commanders made it a living hell. Ten metres away from me, I saw two Germans stab a field nurse with bayonets as she helped a wounded Partisan. The Partisan next to me killed one of them, while I shot the other with a submachine gun. Both fell on top of the dead nurse. My deputy attacked three troopers from behind, they were unable to return fire and all three died. One of our wounded, a Polish man, hid behind a tree and ambushed a German soldier, but the explosion of his hand grenade killed both of them. Two of our machine gunners set up back-to-back and created an arc of fire. They both survived the battle, despite being wounded.

In many post-war memoirs almost all Partisans agreed that their most dangerous opponents were the 7th SS 'Prinz Eugen' Mountain Division composed mainly of the German minority in Yugoslavia. This division caused them many casualties although they tried to avoid engaging it whenever possible. The photo shows a machine-gun nest armed with the murderous MG42 light machine gun.

The Germans employed trained snipers and they were effective. One such sniper killed eight Partisans with shots to the head in the area of Zlatni Bor, and put two machine guns out of action with hits to the weapons.

A standing defence was rarely employed by the Partisans, and only when absolutely unavoidable. Even then, each attack by the enemy would be met with a swift counter-attack. Such defence was employed during the battle to protect the wounded on the River Sutjeska, when the Partisans were surrounded by the Germans. On 6 June 1943, near Gornje Bare, the Dalmatian Brigade and its 600 men held their positions on difficult terrain. They received orders not to retreat and to keep the

position at all costs. The brigade was attacked by the German combat group 'Anaker' comprising some 3,000 soldiers. The core of the group was the 'Brandenburg' battalion and the 118th Jäger Division. It is interesting to note that some 150 Cossacks from the Pinkert Battalion were also in this group: this is the earliest known occurrence of Cossacks fighting on Yugoslav territory. The group attack was supported by 12 German Ju 87 dive-bombers, six artillery batteries and 16 mortars. During the battle, attacks and counter-attacks were constantly exchanged. The German attack was eventually repulsed and one Partisan officer, Branco Milinkovic, has left an account of the battle:

> Night was approaching, and planes and artillery were still hitting the exhausted, reduced battalions which had been fighting off the Germans for two days, resisting them with shelling and counter-attacks. The Germans believed that they had broken the brigade's resistance and the coming night would help them in penetrating the final lines of defence in order to break through to the Sutjeska valley. At about 2100hrs, after an artillery barrage lasting about 30 minutes, averaging 50 shells per minute, the infantry attack began ... It was a terrible battle, with gunshot and explosions echoing all round, and hand-to-hand combat frequent. There were many dead and wounded on both sides.

On that day, the brigade suffered 65 dead and twice as many wounded. The attacks continued with the same intensity for the next three days and three nights, when the Majevica Brigade and its 200 soldiers arrived as reinforcement. Thanks to them, the Dalmatian Brigade held out for one more day, after which it retreated. One hundred and fifty soldiers survived the battle in fighting order. The

Germans were not the only enemy: hunger, typhoid and the lack of supplies and ammunition were equally devastating. Even in the most chaotic of battles, the Partisans succeeded in sometimes capturing the enemy's supply column. A soldier of the 7th Banija Brigade recalls one such success:

At that time, we captured a German supply column of about 50 horses with a large amount of ammunition, as we were almost out of our own. In addition to the regular supplies, we also captured several baskets of lemons. You can imagine what that meant to our soldiers, who for over 11 days had eaten grass, nettles and unsalted horsemeat.

From 1944, the Allied air forces assisted the Partisans by attacking German positions and troops in the Balkans. At times such reinforcements only came at the last minute. In protecting the withdrawal of the General Staff from Drvar on 29 May 1944, the 1st Proletarian Brigade held its position near Lipovac. One soldier, Luka Bozovic, described the attack by a battalion of the 7th SS Division:

With strong artillery support, the SS battalion launched their attack at 1400hrs on the battalion position. The Germans began their attack with a great shout, something they rarely did. We were waiting for them on rocky terrain. We had no ammunition. We had been promised a delivery, but it had not yet arrived from Ribnik. We were ordered to not shoot until the Germans came close. The Germans came so close that they began throwing hand grenades at us. Running out of ammunition, the firing rate of our soldiers dwindled, which the enemy noticed, strengthening their

Among the problems the Partisans faced were parasites and the risk of infection that resulted from a lack of basic hygiene. One of the ways of dealing with this was to boil their uniforms in huge metal barrels.

51

attack. The medical personnel were too few to pull out all the injured fighters from our positions, so the supply staff had to come in and help. When it looked as if there was absolutely no chance left for our side to continue fighting, our soldiers began to prepare to attack with our bayonets. At that moment, nine Allied aircraft flew over our positions and dropped ammunition and food supplies by parachute. The containers fell both on our positions and the German ones. All those in the rear and even the wounded who could still move about participated in gathering up the supplies. The intensity of the battle increased again as our soldiers could return fire.

From autumn 1944, the tactical initiative belonged to the Partisans and not the occupying forces: this meant that attack once again dominated defence.

Ambushes

Ambushes were a common feature of Partisan activity and some units and brigades were renowned for their success in this area. They took place in all types of terrain and weather, by day and by night, and used from groups of no more than a few fighters to those that involved several brigades. To achieve maximum surprise the ambushers often took up their positions fully prepared late at night or early in the morning. Digging-in was not common: each Partisan would take up position, camouflage himself and wait for the order from the officer in charge.

One of the first big ambushes took place not far from Cetinje in Montenegro on 15 July 1941. The Italian Messina Division was attacked and in less than two hours a whole battalion was wiped out without a single Partisan being wounded. With the formation of brigades, divisions and corps the possibilities for preparing ambushes increased and often quite large enemy formations were trapped. For example, in April 1943 near the village of Susnjar in Slavonia, a formation of 2,000 enemy soldiers was destroyed.

Ambushes were highly frustrating for the enemy. They were very expertly placed and in terms of expenditure of ammunition and casualties they were far and away the most successful tactic. There were two kinds of ambush. The first type sought to block or slow down the enemy advance. A good example is the one placed by the Rudar Company in October 1941 on the Krusevac–Kraljevo road where a column of the German 717 Infantry Division was caught. Since there was a shortage of mines, three remote-controlled aircraft bombs were hidden in the bushes on the right side of the road while the fighters were hidden a little further down in the bushes on the left. One surviving account notes:

At the head of the column was a tank followed by about ten lorries full of soldiers. We allowed them to advance until they were all within range of the bomb. There were two loud explosions (a third bomb did not explode). One lorry burst into flames immediately. The Partisans attacked and fought the Germans hand to hand, there were losses on both sides. The Germans organised themselves first where the third bomb had not exploded and opened fire on us and we were forced to retreat.

The second type of ambush was targeted against enemy supply lines and aimed to capture items needed by the Partisans. A typical example is the ambush placed on the Donja–Dubrava–Tounj road in January 1944 by 6th Lika Brigade:

At about 7.30 in the morning four enemy lorries appeared. About 300m behind them were another two. They were carrying food, uniforms and footwear. In each lorry there were 15–20 Domobran troops from Slunj. We opened fire at about 50m, as soon as the first four lorries entered the ambush zone. In a few minutes more than half the enemy were dead or wounded. We opened fire on the last two lorries and the Domobran soldiers ran away immediately.

Forty-six *Domobran* were killed, nine were injured and 41 captured. Two Partisans were slightly wounded. In some ambushes all the enemy soldiers lost their lives: for example in December 1943 the Gradnik Brigade laid an ambush near Hotedrsica for 15 wagons accompanied by 50 German soldiers. In a few minutes all the enemy troops and 28 horses

Captured German soldiers. On the right of the photo is a pile of German uniforms which will be issued to the Partisans. Until 1943 the Germans considered the Partisans to be bandits but when they realised that they were up against an increasingly well organised army they were forced to negotiate with them. One frequent form of negotiation was the exchange of prisoners. A considerable number of Partisans and communists from camps and prisons came out alive in exchange for German soldiers.

had been slaughtered. By the second half of 1943 the Partisans had become so lethal at preparing and executing ambushes that the occupying troops no longer operated in remote areas and increasingly kept themselves to towns and main communication routes, only occasionally executing larger, local offensives.

Anti-tank defence

In the war in Yugoslavia, the Partisans were primarily battling against Italian tanks and captured French tanks operated by German soldiers. These tanks were inferior to the new Allied and German tanks, and were thus used in second-line duty, such as occupation or in training new crews. For the Partisans, who lacked anti-tank weapons, every tank was dangerous. As such, their anti-tank tactics primarily depended on taking advantage of the difficult terrain for these vehicles, disrupting communication between them and setting mines and various obstacles. Throughout the entire war, the Partisans used hand-held anti-tank weapons, such as cluster grenades and petrol bombs in close combat against the tanks. They formed special anti-tank groups several soldiers strong and in practice would use several such units, thus increasing the chances that one of the groups would destroy the tank. The tactic of attacking the tank was simple. One group of soldiers would provide a

A German soldier interrogating prisoners. One of the examiners has given the prisoners cigarettes, probably to relax them and improve the chances of obtaining information.

distraction with gunfire, while a second group would steal up to the tank and attack it. The Partisans would usually withdraw if tanks suddenly appeared in an attack against a village or enemy position, although they sometimes succeeded in fending them off, as was the case in September 1942 when a group encountered three Renault tanks for the first time near the village of Preslica. At first they were bewildered, but one of the soldiers thought to fire fine shot from a hunting rifle into the opening of the tank. The tanks immediately retreated.

In the summer of 1942, the Partisans succeeded in capturing one of the first German 37mm anti-tank guns. The gun came with two horses to pull it, and three horses to carry the grenades. Though they were ordered to destroy the gun in order to advance quicker, the soldiers ignored the orders and, with great difficulty, succeeded in getting out with the gun. The horses all died, but they were quickly replaced. At the last moment, just as they were about to cross the road and vanish into the dense forest, an enemy convoy appeared before them on the road. Heading up the convoy was a black car, followed by a tank: behind that was a lorry and seven additional tanks, followed by another 20 lorries. The Partisans quickly set up the gun and the gunner recalls what happened next:

> I fired the first round at the car and it flipped over into the ditch. I fired the second at the tank, which immediately turned to the right and also went off the road. When an anti-tank round hits metal, it makes a lot of noise, and when it hits the road surface, you can hear the surface and stones exploding into pieces. I stopped another two tanks with the fifth and sixth rounds.

With time, the ambushes and road blocks were better defended with anti-tank guns and properly equipped anti-tank teams. This was important as when the enemy penetrated Partisan territory, they advanced by road with key support provided by tanks. Their attacks too were organised in columns that were headed up by several tanks. The Partisans succeeded in blocking the roads or slowing down the passage of those columns, while managing to destroy a tank or two along the way. As ever, innovation provided extremely effective solutions to the tank issue. In the spring of 1943, a group of soldiers from the Durmitor detachment destroyed an Italian tank by throwing a bag full of explosives onto the tank from a cliff above. The explosives had fuses attached, and the force of the explosion was so great that pieces of the road surface cut through the underside of the tank. Following the capitulation of Italy in September 1943, the Partisans captured a large number of anti-tank guns, thus making their defence more effective. As such, the Germans exercised more caution when using tanks against the Partisans from this point on.

THE END OF THE PARTISANS

With the defeat of the Germany Army and the occupying forces in spring 1945, the quisling states in the territory of Yugoslavia also collapsed. A great number of Ustasha, Chetnik, *Domobran* fighters and members of

Tito with Partisan pilots on the island of Vis. Two fighter-bomber squadrons were equipped with the help of the British.

other police and security formations began to retreat to the west with the German Army. They were followed by a great number of civilians, particularly members of the German minority and officials of the former puppet regimes. At the Austrian border, the Partisans captured over 150,000 people, and separated soldiers and all men suspected to have belonged to the occupying forces. In a long march of almost 700km, they led them to prison camps in Serbia. On this journey, called the 'March of Death', tens of thousands of people were killed or died of exhaustion. Of those who died, the majority were Croats, particularly young men between 17 and 19 who had been mobilised by the NDH regime. Those who succeeded in surviving the prison camps remained second-class citizens with minor political rights until the 1970s.

Following the end of the war, a great number of Partisans remained in the Yugoslav Army due to the crisis with the Allies in Italy over the partitioning of the city of Trieste and part of Istria. The border tension was reduced in 1946–47: Trieste was given to Italy, with part of Istria going to Yugoslavia. However, a new diplomatic crisis soon broke out when Tito refused to obey Stalin, and when the Soviet Union openly threatened to intervene in 1948. Up until 1950, a great number of Partisans remained under arms until this situation too calmed down and those veterans who chose to leave the army could finally return to their homes.

BIBLIOGRAPHY

Bozovic, B., Bajrami, H., Folic, M., and Vavic, M. *Partizanski odredi* (Vojnoizdavacki zavod, Belgrade, 1981)

Grujic, P. *Sesnaesta vojvodjanska brigada* (Vojno delo, Belgrade 1959)

Obradovic *Druga dalmatinska proleterska brigada* (Vojnoizdavacki zavod, Belgrade, 1968)

Pravdic, S. 16. *Slavonska omladinska brigada – Joze Vlahovic* (Vojnoizdavacki zavod, Belgrade, 1976)

Peric, I. *Peta kordunaska brigada* (Vojnoizdavacki zavod, Belgrade, 1972)

Petelin, S. *Gradnikova brigada* (Vojnoizdavacki zavod, Belgrade, 1968)

Seferovic, M. *Trinaesta hercegovacka NOU brigada* (Vojnoizdavacki i novinski centar JNA, Belgrade, 1988)

Vojnoizdavacki i novinski centar – Beograd *Druga krajiska brigada* (Belgrade, 1988)

Vojnoizdavacki i novinski centar – Beograd *Prva proleterska brigada* (Belgrade, 1986)

Vojnoizdavacki zavod – Beograd *15 Majevicka brigada* (Belgrade, 1979)

Vojnoizdavacki zavod – Beograd *Vojna enciklopedija 1–10* (Belgrade, 1971)

Vujasinovic, T. *Ozrenski partizanski odred*

COLOUR PLATE COMMENTARY

A: SLOVENE PARTISAN, LIBERATION FRONT, 1942

The illustration shows a Slovene Partisan (1), a member of the Liberation Front of 1942. He can be distinguished by the colours of the Slovene tricolour below the star on his cap. The Slovene cap had a distinctive three-pointed top and was known as the 'Triglav cap' after Slovenia's highest mountain with its three peaks (2). In the spring of 1942 Partisans all over Yugoslavia adopted this from Croatian Partisans, it had originally been brought over by anti-Facists who had fought in the Spanish Civil War. It was widely worn until the beginning of 1944 when the so-called 'Tito cap' took its place.

The Partisan wears a short, civilian coat with wide, fashionable collars and two rows of buttons. He is armed with a Yugoslav M24 Mauser 7.92mm calibre rifle. They were made on licence granted by the Belgian Fabrique Nationale d'Armes de Guerre and were produced in Kragujevac in Serbia. On his belt he carries the M35 hand grenade and a large ammunition pouch for the famous 37 Zbroyovka machine gun produced in Kragujevac under Czech licence.

In September 1941 the Supreme Headquarters prescribed that Partisans in all of Yugoslavia should wear an anti-Fascist red star attached to their caps (3). Soon afterwards the Supreme Headquarters of the Slovene Partisan detachments issued its own regulations prescribing (as a symbol of the Slovene Partisans) a national three-coloured flag, here seen as two different types of badge (4), 4cm long and 2cm wide with a red five-pointed star of 3cm diameter in the middle. These badges were made of tin, secretly produced in Ljubljana and delivered to the Partisans.

The 1st Proletarian Brigade (according to communist ideology the brigade was made up of members of the working class) was founded in Eastern Bosnia on 21 December 1941. The aim was that larger formations would be created from the best fighters who (unlike other Partisans) would not be identified with a fixed territory but would be ready to fight anywhere in Yugoslavia. The 1st Proletarian Brigade had 1,199 fighters of whom 651 were Communist Party members. The brigade flag was red (5) with a yellow hammer and sickle, the symbol of the international workers' movement. From April 1942 all Partisans in Proletarian Brigades were ordered to wear a hammer and sickle on their star (6).

At the beginning of March 1942 the Supreme Headquarters introduced the first insignia and rank indicators which were worn on the left arm. The star was 3cm long and the ribbons below it were 6cm long and 1.5cm wide. The ranks were: Corporal (7), Sergeant (8), Company Commander (9), Battalion Commander (10), Detachment Commander (11), Brigade Commander or Group Commander (12). Political commissars wore identical insignia except for the star with the hammer and sickle in the middle. This distinction caused a dispute with the Christian Socialists, members of the

A group of Partisans wearing Yugoslav Army and Croatian *Domobran* uniforms taken in 1942. Only later when they began to fight the Germans more intensively did German uniforms appear among those worn by the Partisans.

Liberation Front of Slovenia, who complained that the communists were trying to turn the Partisan army into a Communist Party army. Slovene headquarters authorised the commissars of Slovenia to have an OF (Liberation Front) inscribed in the middle of the star. It is little known that in Yugoslavia the first decorations of merit in the National Liberation War went to Slovene Partisans. Slovene Headquarters introduced in June 1942 three decorations: a bravery distinction (not shown), the Order of Slovene Liberation Flag (not shown) and the Order of the Partisan star (13). The bravery award was to be worn on the left sleeve, while the other two were on the left breast. The decorations were made of felt and embroidered in gold.

The Partisans' skill in improvising weapons was especially evident in their hand grenades (14, 15, 16). 15 was made from iron piping and from converted Italian 45mm mortar grenades. They favoured the M35 hand grenades (16) produced in Kragujevac in a number of variants, these they later made themselves.

In the middle of 1942 the Slovene Partisans managed to produce a gun (17) which they named 'the Turjak cannon' and which was used against the Italians in Iska Vas in July of the same year. It was made from a tube taken from an old

An identification booklet with the name Zlata Rumina 1943. Since there were no photographs, these documents gave a description of the person. The description in this booklet is: size – small, face – round, eyes – blue, mouth – normal, moustache – none. In the section for weapons is written 'pistol calibre 6.35mm'.

Yugoslav trench mortar of 81cm calibre, bolted onto a wooden frame. The whole structure had a chassis-like base. Its shells (17a) were reconstructed Italian aircraft bombs weighing from 2–3kg. The trigger was taken from a rifle.

B: TRAINING TO USE THE M15 GUN, SUMMER 1944

In the first three years of the war the Partisans captured guns and used them until their ammunition ran out or until they had to retreat: they would then bury or destroy them. The Partisans adopted a mobile method of warfare and guns were often an encumbrance. In February 1943 they defeated the Italian Murge Division and captured 100 of its guns which they were forced to throw into the Neretva River as they could not find a way to take them with them. Knowing that the Partisans did not have artillery the occupation forces set up strongpoints intended for defence against light infantry arms. In small villages a solid defence position could be constructed of several adjacent stone houses which, if the Partisans broke through the outer line of defence, could be held by a small force until reinforcements reached them. The Partisans' failure to take well-fortified and defended places was caused by their lack of artillery. This situation changed radically in the second half of 1943. When Italy capitulated the Partisans were able to take a considerable number of their mountain guns (Skoda M 75mm model 15, which the Italians called Obice 75/13) and several thousand mules to transport them. In order to avoid being captured by the Germans a large number of Italians joined the Partisans, including a lot of experienced gunners. With their help a number of Partisan batteries that at first had had only one or two guns became well armed.

This illustration shows the Partisan crew of six training to use an M15 gun in the summer of 1944. There are a number of curious onlookers in the distance. Among the crew there may well have been an Italian gunner wearing Partisan uniform. One Partisan beside the gun is holding a small instruction manual. The crew is standing in order of firing, the first is taking a shell from a case, the second setting the fuse. There was always the possibility that a training exercise might suddenly become a real battle and so firing drill had to be mastered as soon as possible. The basics were learned and the rest mastered during real fighting.

C: WEAPONS

Until 1944, when the Partisans began to receive more sophisticated Allied weapons and ammunition, they fought a guerrilla war in which rifles and hand grenades were the main weapons. Their chief adversaries at this time were various quisling formations whose weapons varied greatly: they had very few automatic weapons and what they had was usually old.

Not until the beginning of 1943 did a considerable number of well-armed German units begin to fight an anti-guerrilla war in the Balkans. The Partisans' main source of guns and automatic weapons was what they managed to capture from the enemy. Light machine guns were particularly valued but were difficult to come by. Lack of ammunition was a chronic problem and the difficulties were increased by the number of different calibres needed; the most commonly used on the Yugoslav battlefield were Italian 6.5 and 8mm, German 7.92mm, Soviet 7.62mm and British 7.7mm. It is of interest that the first brigades founded in 1942 had an average of 800–900 rifles, 20–30 heavy and light machine guns and 40–50 cartridges per Partisan

soldier which was hardly sufficient for an attack against any sizeable enemy position. Any attack that failed would put a brigade out of action until it was able to capture another supply of ammunition. Careful management of ammunition was one of the basic principles of Partisan warfare, which clashed with the use of automatic weapons. Not until the second half of the war did ammunition become more plentiful. The rare sub-machine guns were used by couriers or at headquarters for close-range defence. Below is a list of commonly used Partisan weapons:

1. Partisanka, cal. 7.92mm, magazine 5 rounds. For the needs of the pre-war Yugoslav Army the factory in Uzica produced M24 Mausers under a Belgian licence from Fabrique Nationale d'Armes de Guerre. When Uzica was liberated in 1941 fully operational machines and tools fell into Partisan hands and before they were forced to retreat they had managed to produce 16,500 Mausers (known as Partisanka – the feminine form of the word Partisan) very similar to the German Gewehr 98 rifle. An interesting footnote is that several thousand of these were given to the Chetniks in the hope that they would use them against the Germans.

2. Kar 98k, cal. 7.92mm, magazine 5 rounds. The standard rifle of the German Army in World War II was the Mauser Gewehr 98 (1898) and a shortened version that appeared in 1935, the Kar 98k. This carbine was produced in Yugoslavia also under the mark M24 CK and was thus widely known. The Kar 98k was solidly made and reliable and for this reason was highly regarded by the Partisans.

3. Mosin-Nagant M1944, cal. 7.62mm, magazine 5 rounds. The agreement with Moscow concerning arming the Partisans began to come into force in the summer of 1944 and included this carbine with permanently attached folding bayonet. As a result of Soviet aid the Partisans in the second half of 1944 were able to form 71 new brigades in Serbia and Macedonia alone.

4. Carcano M1891/38, cal. 6.5mm, magazine 5 rounds. This was the standard Italian rifle large numbers of which were captured by the Partisans. Compared with other European ammunition the Italian cartridge calibre 6.5mm was much less powerful and travelled a much smaller distance. This did not worry the Partisans too much because they mainly attacked by night and at close range.

5. Carcano M1891, cal. 6.5mm, magazine 6 rounds. The Italian carbine which at the end of the 19th century had been mainly produced for the cavalry became the standard infantry weapon in World War II. Because of its short length of only 920mm (36.2in.) and weight of 3kg (106oz) it became the favourite weapon of couriers of whom a large number were boys.

6. Bren Mk II, cal. 7.7mm, magazine 30 rounds. The famous British Bren gun was based on the Czech light machine gun Zbroyovka ZB 30. In the Yugoslav armaments factory in Kragujevac a slightly older model of the Zbroyovka ZB 27 was produced under licence as the M37. Czech construction was very well understood in Yugoslavia and used by all sides. There was a large Partisan base on the

A photo of training in the use of a mountain gun taken somewhere in Dalmatia in the summer of 1944. Due to the difficult passage through the mountains, mules and donkeys were the only possible means of transportation. In order to transport a single cannon with its ammunition, six or seven animals were required. As a rule, each animal was led by one Partisan who would care for it.

island of Vis which was used by British commandos and torpedo boats. One of the best-armed Partisan units was established there (the 26th Dalmatian Division) for which the British provided weapons and uniforms. This division alone had 2,000 Lee Enfield rifles, 300 Bren light machine guns, and several artillery units armed with the 6-pdr and 25-pdr guns.

7. PPsh 41, cal. 7.62mm, magazine 35–71 rounds. Following the Red Army model, from the end of 1944 the Partisans formed infantry companies entirely armed with these Soviet submachine guns.

8. MG34, cal. 7.92mm, belt feed. This excellent German automatic weapon could be used as a heavy machine gun or as a light machine gun. Every captured MG34 and the later and better MG42 was a great prize for it greatly improved the firepower of any unit.

9. Beretta Modello 38A, cal. 9mm, magazine 10, 20 and 30 rounds. This Italian sub-machine gun was a high-quality product. After Italy capitulated a large number were captured. Until the end of the war they continued to be captured from the Germans and other *Domobran* units who had themselves captured them from the Italians.

D: A PARTISAN AMBUSH

The main illustration shows an ambush by 20 Partisans of the 5th Kordun Brigade in summer 1944. They are armed with two heavy machine guns (Schwarzlose MG05 [1] and

Maxim MG08 [2]) aimed at two lorries (only one shown) of an Ustasha patrol. In a few minutes 14 of the enemy were killed, 17 wounded and two Ustasha captured. Both lorries were destroyed. In spite of surprise the Ustasha managed to partly return fire and one machine gunner was wounded.

The inset illustration shows characteristic ambush positions. Three Partisans form the gun crew of a heavy German Maxim MG08 7.92mm machine gun. On the march one crew member carries the gun, the second the tripod and the third the ammunition. The illustration shows the ammunition in canvas bags (3). There were always two reserve crews of three for each gun and if the first crew was killed the next would take over and continue the fight. In cases when retreat was inevitable the gun crews would withdraw first, protected by the rest of the unit.

The Ustasha had several armoured cars and tanks but in one-day action or patrols at longer distance they would go by lorry. The Daimler-Benz L 3000 lorry in the illustration is characteristically filled with 20 soldiers armed with three Maxim MG08 machine guns ready for firing. One is aimed forwards, the other two right and left. In the top left corner there is a diagram showing the most common forms of ambush with the Partisans (red) on the road waiting for the enemy (blue). The red arrows indicate Partisan troop movement. The different forms were:

4. An ambush on one side of the road only.

5. An ambush on both sides was more effective but the danger was that the Partisans might hit their own side.

6. Alternate ambushes were staggered on either side of a road to prevent casualties from one's own side.

7. A frontal ambush was used to make a road impassable.

8. An ambush in the enemy rear to prevent his withdrawal.

9. A horseshoe ambush was the most effective. It sealed the enemy in a closed trap. This kind of ambush needed a high level of training and experience.

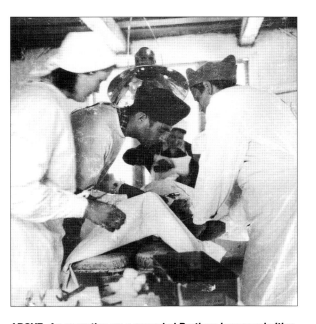

ABOVE An operation on a wounded Partisan in very primitive conditions. Because of the shortage of anaesthetics, patients often had to be tied to the table and the amputations carried out on them when they were fully conscious.

10. An ambush activated after the head of the column had passed. This form was used to attack larger columns of troops.

E: LIVING IN THE WOODS

The illustration shows a group of Partisans round a fire in the woods in late autumn 1944. A number of them have new coats captured from enemy stores. They have put their weapons aside and are eating; one of them is trying to get some sleep. The two officers share the food and fire with the men. A sentry has joined them but he still has his rifle slung over his shoulder. This scene was typical for the whole war all over Yugoslavia. At times when there was fighting going on it was often forbidden to light fires especially at night, as they might give away the Partisan positions to the enemy. Note how this fire has been built to produce little smoke. The men would then huddle together for warmth and try to get a little sleep. They would light their first fire at dawn taking care not to burn wet leaves or grass which would make a lot of smoke. The wood they had to use was usually wet and burned with difficulty: for this reason the Partisans always carried a little dry wood with them to get the fire going.

BELOW Two Partisans posing in front of the camera with a German 81mm Gr. W. 34 mortar. The Allies gave the Partisans large amounts of captured German and Italian weaponry. This mortar had probably been captured in Africa or southern Italy.

Partisans with captured Italian L6 tanks in Split, November 1943. When news arrived of the Italian capitulation, 15,000 townspeople disarmed the Italian garrison and Bergamo Division on 9 October 1943. Until 26 October the town repulsed German attacks, after which the defendants were forced to withdraw into the hills.

F: ASSAULT ON AN ITALIAN PILLBOX

As a result of ever more frequent Partisan successes, especially at the beginning of 1943, the Italians kept themselves to the larger villages which they surrounded with minefields and barbed wire and fortified with concrete pillboxes. Such defensive positions were cleverly built and were difficult to take: the entire surrounding area was covered by gunfire. A special 'Italian' feature was hanging tins and cans on the barbed wire, which rattled at the least touch to the wire. Wandering donkeys, sheep and strong winter winds would sometimes provoke a hail of Italian machine-gun fire.

Being short of artillery a key Partisan weapon was the hand grenade. The bravest young led the way: many were blown up by their own grenades. Such attacks usually took place in the dark. Partisans would crawl up to the enemy positions finding a way through the minefields and barbed wire hoping to get as far as possible without being discovered.

The illustration shows a group of Partisans attacking an Italian pillbox by day having managed to get through the outer defences at night. The pillboxes were connected to each other by stone walls: the stony ground made it almost impossible to dig trenches. The Partisans would attack a number of pillboxes at once because they protected each other with crossfire. This group of Partisans is no longer in danger of coming under fire from the neighbouring pillbox and has managed to secure a blind spot where they cannot be seen by the enemy gunners. One of the grenadiers has been killed by his own grenade, which was thrown back at him by the Italian crew before it exploded in the pillbox. Another throws grenades at the pillbox. A third Partisan is covering the area to the right of the pillbox in case any enemy should come from that direction. A fourth watches out for Italians appearing from another pillbox. A fifth has been killed before he had a chance to ignite his grenade. A sixth is encouraging other Partisans to go forward.

G: MOUNT ZELENGORA, JUNE 1943

Among the major anti-Partisan operations was the Fifth offensive, codenamed 'Operation Schwartz' by the Germans, which lasted from 15 May to 15 June in the valley of the River Sutjeska. It witnessed one of the decisive battles of the war in Yugoslavia. A force of 70,000 Germans, 43,000 Italians, 10,000 anti-Partisan Yugoslav troops, and 2,000 Bulgarians surrounded and gradually closed in on the Supreme Headquarters: Tito, four Partisan divisions and a number of independent brigades were located there, totalling 16,000 combat-ready Partisans and some 4,000 sick and wounded. The fighting reached its peak when for almost two days six brigades defended a pass only 4km wide through which the main body of the Partisan army was retreating, led by the 1st Proletarian Brigade. They were being pursued from behind by the German 1st Mountain Division, and pressed on the left by the 7th SS 'Prinz Eugen' Division, the 118th Jäger Division, the 369th Devil's Division and the Italian Taurinese Division. The trap was closed by two battalions of the 369th Division on Mount Zelengora. The Partisans were shelled and bombed from the air on a daily basis. Attack and counter-attack took place on the mountain peaks, and the Partisans suffered heavy casualties. A brigade originally of about 800–1,000 men was reduced to no more than 200. Constant fighting, hunger and typhoid fever decimated the Partisan ranks. The end seemed near and the enemy decided that on 10 June they would make a concerted attack and bring about the final defeat of Tito's forces. Faced with this situation it was decided in the evening of 9 June, in the headquarters of the 1st Proletarian Brigade, that they would attack the positions of the 369th Division on Mount Zelengora. Early in the morning of 10 June the Proletarian Brigade attacked and managed to break through the enemy encirclement. They were followed by the other brigades and the main column. The central hospital with the wounded was in the rear of the column and was cut off and surrounded by the Germans. The 3rd Division was destroyed defending the wounded, about 1,000 of whom were butchered by the enemy. Some in small groups managed to escape over Mount Zelengora.

The illustration shows a group of exhausted and hungry Partisans on Zelengora after a month of constant marching and fighting. They have paused in the shelter of a large tree for a short rest.

H: MACHINE GUNNERS OF THE VOJVODINA BRIGADE AND HERCEGOVINA BRIGADE, SPRING 1944

In the summer of 1944 the Soviet Army was approaching the eastern borders of Yugoslavia, threatening Axis Army Group E in Greece that was there to oppose any Allied invasion threat in the Balkans. The only suitable way to withdraw these troops was through Serbia, down the lower course of the Vardar, through Nis and Belgrade and eastwards. In the summer of 1944 Tito decided to march with several divisions from Bosnia into Serbia. The German supreme command in the Balkans responded by engaging a large force to prevent their advance. Despite a number of exhausting and heavy battles, the Partisan divisions managed to advance through Montenegro into Serbia in September. The 16th Vojvodina Brigade from Eastern Bosnia and the 11th Hercegovina Brigade took part in these battles. Unlike earlier Partisan battles this one was fought with Allied air support in the form of transport planes from Italy that flew almost every night. Using radio communication they located Partisan units and parachuted them supplies and ammunition. The planes brought food to improvised airstrips and on their return journeys took out the sick and wounded. The items featured on this illustration are:

1. A machine gunner of the Vojvodina Brigade in spring 1944 armed with an MG34. This gun weighed 12kg and only strong men could carry it. It was a special honour to be entrusted with this gun and loss of it meant a military court marshal. Many of the gunners became legendary, their names were known far and wide: if a unit entered a village then almost at once the tall, burly gunners were the centre of attention – though this also made them an easy target to spot, and an important one to eliminate. The Partisans called the MG34 and MG42 *sarac* and said they could tell each one from the sound it made when it was fired.

The gunner in the picture has a German cloth tunic cut in green twill with six buttons and officer's breeches and jackboots. His cap has been made in a local workshop. He has a standard belt with 50 rounds of ammunition and on his belt he carries a vz38 Czech pistol and an M17 Yugoslav hand grenade.

2. A sub-machine gunner of the 11th Hercegovina Brigade, summer 1944, armed with a Beretta M38 sub-machine gun. In spring 1944, especially in Dalmatia and Hercegovina, large quantities of British uniforms began to arrive. The Partisan in this illustration is wearing brand new British khaki battledress. The British battledress jacket was very popular among the Partisans. On his head he wears a forage cap known as a Tito cap, or *Titovka*, made from British material according to Tito's order of April 1944, by which this became the official Partisan cap. He is carrying a Beretta with the largest magazine, containing 30 rounds. Attached to his waist is a British Mills No. 36M grenade.

3. In August 1943 Partisan medals were instituted, designed by the well-known sculptor August Augustincic. From summer 1944 they were produced in the Soviet Union. The illustration shows the Order of the Partisan Star First Class won for leadership skills and special merit in battle. After the liberation of Belgrade in 1944 a large number of medals were presented at a military parade.

4. Order of Bravery Medal for bravery shown during the War of National Liberation.

5. Throughout the war the Partisans tried to manufacture guns themselves. In October 1944 the Slovenian Partisans produced a gun that was called the *partop*. The barrel was taken from an 81mm mortar. The shell was made from tin and filled with three to five kilograms of N808 explosive. The mine weighed 9.5kg to 12.5kg. The total empty weight of the *partop* was 59kg. It was a very powerful gun and could penetrate a 50cm wall leaving a hole of 120cm diameter. Its range was 200m.

A Partisan officer in November 1944 proudly showing the Order of Bravery medal on his new uniform. In the Soviet Union from August 1944 orders, cap medals and metal uniform buttons were made for the Partisans in Yugoslavia.

INDEX

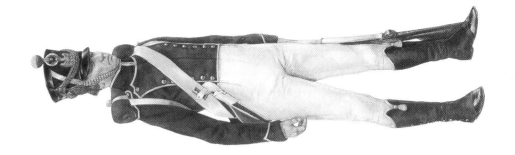

FIND OUT MORE ABOUT OSPREY

❏ Please send me the latest listing of Osprey's publications

❏ I would like to subscribe to Osprey's e-mail newsletter

Title/rank

Name

Address

Postcode/zip   state/country

e-mail

I am interested in:

❏ Ancient world
❏ Medieval world
❏ 16th century
❏ 17th century
❏ 18th century
❏ Napoleonic
❏ 19th century

❏ American Civil War
❏ World War I
❏ World War II
❏ Modern warfare
❏ Military aviation
❏ Naval warfare

Please send to:

USA & Canada:
Osprey Direct USA, c/o MBI Publishing, P.O. Box 1, 729 Prospect Avenue, Osceola, WI 54020

UK, Europe and rest of world:
Osprey Direct UK, P.O. Box 140, Wellingborough, Northants, NN8 2FA, United Kingdom

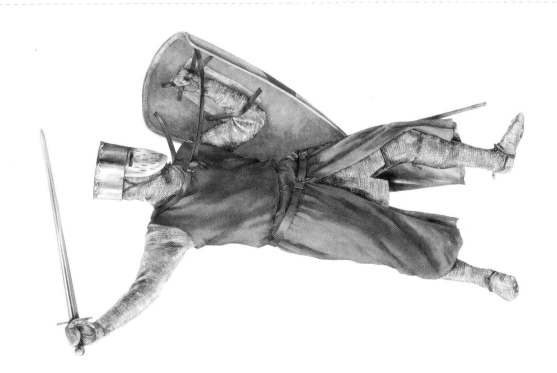

OSPREY
PUBLISHING

www.ospreypublishing.com

call our telephone hotline
for a free information pack

USA & Canada: 1-800-826-6600
UK, Europe and rest of world call:
+44 (0) 1933 443 863

Young Guardsman
Figure taken from *Warrior 22:*
Imperial Guardsman 1799–1815
Published by Osprey
Illustrated by Christa Hook

Knight, c.1190
Figure taken from *Warrior 1: Norman Knight 950 – 1204 AD*
Published by Osprey
Illustrated by Christa Hook

POSTCARD